The Journey of "OLD FREMONT"

A REVOLUTIONARY WAR RIFLE

Col. Joe L. Martin

iUniverse, Inc.
Bloomington

The Journey of "Old Fremont"
A Revolutionary War Rifle

iUniverse books may be ordered through booksellers or by contacting:

iUniverse
1663 Liberty Drive
Bloomington, IN 47403
www.iuniverse.com
1-800-Authors (1-800-288-4677)

Because of the dynamic nature of the Internet, any Web addresses or
links contained in this book may have changed since publication and
may no longer be valid. The views expressed in this work are solely those
of the author and do not necessarily reflect the views of the publisher,
and the publisher hereby disclaims any responsibility for them.

Any people depicted in stock imagery provided by Thinkstock are models,
and such images are being used for illustrative purposes only.

Certain stock imagery © Thinkstock.

ISBN: 978-1-4759-8431-6 (sc)
ISBN: 978-1-4759-8432-3 (e)

Library of Congress Control Number: 2013906847

Printed in the United States of America

iUniverse rev. date: 4/12/2013

DEDICATED TO LINDA

For love of family, genealogy, and travel.
Also, dedicated to the young people of all families.
I fervently hope it will inspire them to
search for their roots.

$\mathcal{C}$ONTENTS

CHAPTER ONE

STORYTELLER

In each family there is one who seems called to find the ancestors, to put flesh on their bones and make them live again, to tell the family story and to feel that somehow the ancestors know and approve.

Exploring genealogy is not a cold gathering of facts but, instead, breathing life into all who has gone before. We are the storytellers of the tribe. All tribes have one. Our genes have called us, as it were. Those who have gone before cry out: "Tell our story!" So, we do. In finding them, we somehow find ourselves. How many graves have I now stood over and cried? I have lost count. How many times have I told the ancestors, "You have a wonderful family; you would be proud of us."

CHAPTER TWO

FOREWORD

It has been said through history, "If you last, it's a mystery." So begins the mystery of Old Fremont, a Revolutionary War Kentucky flintlock rifle, now resting quietly in the Lakeport County museum in California.

Yes, a Revolutionary War rifle in California. As if liberating a new nation wasn't enough, Old Fremont was not content to sit idle. Treasured by caring hands, it provided food and safe passage to this westward-bound family, across the continent to settle in another new frontier.

Americans often reflect on the people, ingenuity and milestones that have contributed to our freedom. Old Fremont deserves recognition not only for lasting the course of history but for what its design represents in the context of the American Revolution.

History tells us that the Brown Bess Rifle/

Musket was standard issue for British infantry and the convention by which it ruled. It could be loaded quickly and fire just about anything a soldier could stuff down its oversized barrel. A large, black-powder charge was required to fire this short-barreled musket. This became highly inefficient and led to chronic fouling of the barrel and touch hole. The design accounted for this fouling by using undersized projectiles which clumsily exited the barrel with little stability or accuracy. The barrels had one forward sight and no rear sight, much like a shotgun. These limitations determined 18th century battle tactics, which employed long lines of men trained for speed of loading rather than accuracy.

By contrast, one of the earliest forms of American ingenuity, the Kentucky rifle, also commonly referred to as the Pennsylvania long rifle, became a design that forever changed the world of this young nation. German and Swiss craftsmen in Pennsylvania are credited with discovering that the round lead ball fired from muskets could be stabilized, providing greater range and accuracy by machining "rifled" barrels much longer than those of the Brown Bess musket.

The "rifling" or grooves machined in a continuous helical spiral within the barrel put a spin on the ball much the way a football is spiraled through the air with greater accuracy as opposed to being kicked or pushed through the air. The longer, rifled barrel combined with a smaller caliber, more slender stock, rear sight, more efficiently sized round balls and much less black powder proved decisive on Revolutionary War battlefields and beyond.

The many intricate technical innovations of the design of the Old Fremont Kentucky long rifle and the crucial timing in history during which it was deployed embodies freedom as we know it.

The value of Old Fremont to its owners is evident by its remarkable condition now over two hundred years of freedom later. They knew Old Fremont was the one thing they could count on to feed and protect them.

Consider this incredible historical journey through the sights of Old Fremont as it liberated a nation, tamed a continent and provided for families moving westward.

Daniel (Dan) A. Martin
Round Mountain, California

CHAPTER THREE

PREFACE

As family historians, we initially find our ancestors through family members, research and travel. For some, we are unable to learn much about. We would like to learn more, such as where and how they lived. What they thought did and felt about family and life in general. If we find something written about them, or even better, written by them, we feel really lucky as we do if we happen upon any likeness of them—picture or photo.

I think at one time or another we all have wished we could jump into a time machine and travel to places of our ancestors' past, and meet them. We would ask them for the answers we can't find, our research, in libraries, Bible records, and archives-especially those middle initials that elude us so often.

For many generations our ancestors would have seen little change during their lives, possibly plowing that one acre a day. The Industrial Revolution made the difference and more recently change seems to have gone exponential.

Memories, we all have them; some make us happy—some make us sad. Some we are ready to share, with others not to be relived with anyone. But what else can they be? They can be someone else's history. Children's history lessons can include topics that we have lived through. Even some-thing ordinary and mundane to us, the facts can be of interest to others.

We are in the age of the computer chip, communications and information. With the speed of the change in the area of technology, the iPod or cell phone is out of date only a few days after taken out of the box! Telegraph, telephone, iphone, radio, television, HD, 3D, desktop, touchpad—where will it lead to next?

The overland Santa Fe Wagon train story and the journey of "Old Fremont", an old Revolutionary War Rifle and the ancestors of that generation; how it reached its final destination in California, is about this time change. It seems too far away in time but it's only a flash within our human history and time.

Col. Joe L. Martin, USAF (Ret.)

CHAPTER FOUR

DEAR ANCESTOR

Your tombstone stands among the rest
In this field of green
The name and date are chiseled out
It reaches out to all who care;
It is too late to mourn
You died before I was born.
Yet we are of one, you and me,
In flesh, in blood, in bone,
Our blood contracts and beats a pulse
Entirely not our own.
The life you lived almost two hundred
Years ago spreads out among the ones
You left, who would have loved you
So I wonder if you lived and loved, I
wonder If you knew, that someday I
would find This spot and come visit you.
(Author Unknown)

CHAPTER FIVE

INTRODUCTION

By Colonel Joe Martin

The Journey of Old Fremont
In Commemoration of Major Brice Martin

The epic story of one family's journey on the Santa Fe Trail from Missouri to California was of the journey leaving Missouri in 1853, hoping for a better life. Old Fremont, the Revolutionary war rifle traveled with Martin Hammack from New Hope, Missouri beginning its history in Virginia during the Revolutionary War, then went to Tennessee, Missouri and finally over the Santa Fe Trail in a train of 13 wagons led by Wagon Master, Martin Hammack, to Lake County California, arriving in April 1854. The Revolutionary War rifle is now on display at the Lakeport County Museum in Lakeport, California.

This brief history relates facts known about the

rifle. It also gives detailed historical accounts of two families, the Martins and the Hammacks, who are closely tied together by friendship and marriage.

The rifle was originally owned by Major Brice Martin, the brother of General Joseph Martin, who later gave it to Martin Hammack. John Hammack Sr., his father, served and died in the American Revolution. After his death, John's wife Mary Martin Hammack, otherwise known as "Nellie" and her three sons, Martin, Brice and John Jr., moved to the beautiful state of Tennessee. Nellie's grandson, Daniel Hammack, who married Mary "Polly" are both buried in Cato, Smith County, Tennessee, in the Colonel William Lucas Martin Cemetery.

Mary "Polly Martin" Hammack was a sister of Colonel William Lucas Martin and the daughter of General Joseph Martin, Jr.

Major Brice Martin served first as a captain, following as major, during the American Revolution, along with his brothers, General Joseph, Ensign John Martin Sr., and Captain William Martin during many of the Indian uprisings before, during and after the Revolution. The areas in which they served were Virginia, North Carolina, South Carolina, Georgia and Tennessee. All of the brothers served at Martin's Station near Cumberland Gap, Tennessee and other frontier forts, such as Long Island, General Joseph Martin's Cherokee Agency Headquarters.

Major Brice Martin was one of the distinguished Colonial military officers and a son of Captain Joseph

Martin, Sr., the immigrant to America who sailed from England to Virginia in about 1725 aboard a family owned ship called the "Brice." Captain Joseph Martin Sr. put down roots in Virginia after marrying Susannah Chiles, the daughter of the prominent and wealthy Chiles family of Jamestown.

Their descendants can be found today in over 40 states, and one family in England.

This story also tells of the hardships which the Hammack families encountered when migrating from New Hope, Lincoln County, Missouri, departing in April 1853. Traveling across the plains in 13 covered wagons on the Santa Fe Trail, the journey took six months before reaching their final destination in April 1854 in the beautiful valley of Lake County, California. They suffered many hardships of fatigue, sickness, death, hunger, extreme hot weather, homesickness, roving western Indian bands and much more. With much faith and strife, they finally reached their final destination with only two deaths. They buried the bodies late at night so the roving bands of Indians would not discover the graves. Hammack descendants can be found today in California, Oregon, Tennessee, Missouri and Kentucky.

This book is an outgrowth of time and many years spent administering valuable family research. My main objective in writing this history of these families and the Revolutionary War rifle is for present, and hopefully instill in our future descendants a pride of having ancestors who strived for a better life for their children and grandchildren. I began my genealogy and family research in 1972, although I had thought about it most of my adult life. The research became so interesting, I have continued it ever since and now have much of our family history back to 1066AD. To me, there is nothing more interesting and so fascinating, at least none that offers rich rewards in proportion as historical research. To follow an elusive historical trail or event and capture the truth and make it my own brings a real satisfaction I would not trade for anything. It brings a great value of being mine forever to share with others, without fear of loss. With the help of my wife, Linda, a great historian and genealogist in her own right, we worked tirelessly on many travels and combed through documents of state, county and public collections throughout several states while researching my family and their history. I owe my debt to several institutions and individuals. Some have been named but not all; many I have forgotten. The main source of information has come from the many courthouses, state archives, cemeteries, and families, people I have met while traveling thousands of miles conducting personal interviews while doing research for the historical facts of our families. While performing research in Tennessee in 2003, I discovered information about Major Brice Martin's Revolutionary War rifle and its long and dangerous journey to California with the Martin Hammack wagon train. The rifle was researched and after several months it was found in the Lake County Museum, at Lakeport, California. The rifle was given to the museum by a descendant of Martin Hammack, Ms. Clara Woods, in 1929. More research about the rifle's history followed and today we know some of its history. The old rifle now has a final resting place in its own special display case, thanks to Lake County, California.

Finally, after months of research, I determined that the rifle belonged to Major Brice Martin, a Revolutionary War officer and son of Captain Joseph Martin, Sr. my fifth great grandfather. Major Brice Martin's brother General Joseph Martin Jr. was the famous hero of the southern frontier. He was also the Cherokee Indian Agent for the Centennial Congress, North Carolina, Virginia, and Virginia Representative. He was Henry County's first general officer, who Martinsville, Virginia, was named for in 1791.

We owe a great amount of gratitude to our early pioneer ancestors mentioned in these pages. I especially want to thank the late Ms. Clara Woods Rivers who had the foresight and vision to donate the rifle to the Museum many years ago, which belonged to both our Martin and Hammack ancestors. It is my hope the Martin and Hammack descendants will continue the research and keep the family history alive for our children and grandchildren.

CHAPTER SIX

LAKE COUNTY MUSEUM

The rifle was donated to the museum in 1929 by Ms. Clara Woods Rivers, a granddaughter of Martin Hammack. It was first owned by Major Brice Martin of Martinsville, Virginia, and used during the Revolutionary War.

It was given to Martin Hammack and used for his safety, during the long journey from Missouri to California in 1853. Martin Hammack also used the rifle in the War of 1812 and the Black Hawk Indian War of 1832.

While researching the rifle, it had to be determined which Brice Martin actually owned the rifle first. To do this, I had to sort out the different Brice Martins who could have owned the rifle. Martin was a popular name, including the name Brice Martin.

Major Brice Martin, who owned the rifle first in Virginia, gave it to Martin Hammack, perhaps first to his nephew, another Major Brice Martin in Smith County, Tennessee, then he gave it to Martin Hammack, who was preparing for a journey to California in 1853. Martin Hammack took the rifle on a 13-wagon train to California.

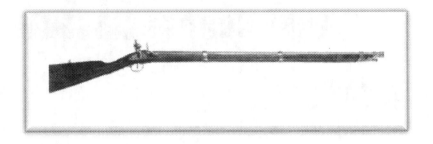

CHAPTER SEVEN

OLD FREMONT

This Revolutionary War rifle nicknamed "Old Fremont" belonged to Major Brice Martin and was used by him before, during and following the Revolutionary War. The rifle was later given to his nephew, another Major Brice Martin of Smith County, and then he gave it to Martin Hammack. Martin, a soldier in General Andrew Jackson's Army, used this rifle in the Battle of New Orleans, War of 1812 and in the Black Hawk Indian War of 1832. Martin Hammack carried this rifle with him on the long journey across the plains, desert and mountains from New Hope (Lincoln County), Missouri, to Lake County, California. Eventually the rifle was given to the Lake County Museum in 1929 by Clara (Woods) Rivers, a granddaughter of Martin Hammack.

The bayonet which was attached to the rifle and likewise used during both the Revolutionary War and War of 1812 was owned by Harold M. Hammack of Riverside, California. The whereabouts of the bayonet is unknown today and no contact has been found for this family.

The Kentucky Long Rifle is thought to have been made in Pennsylvania or Maryland. The stock of the rifle is made of maple and was originally a flintlock that was later changed to a percussion lock.

The rifle was used in the American Revolution by Major Brice Martin. Pictured holding the rifle is Colonel Joe L. Martin, a fourth great-nephew of Major Brice Martin.

Martin Hammack, a soldier in Andrew Jackson's Army, used this rifle in the British War Battle of New Orleans of 1812, and in the Black Hawk Indian War of 1832.

The rifle was taken to California in 1853, when Martin Hammack, who was Captain of the Hammack Party wagon train, and his son, Brice Hammack went to California with their families and settled in Lake County. They were the first white settlers to settle in Big Valley, Lake County in 1854.

Colonel Joe L. Martin with Major Brice
Martin's 1774–1775 Revolutionary rifle.

CHAPTER EIGHT

AMERICAN LONG RIFLE

In Europe, where many firearms were made for royalty and gentry, with exquisite craftsmanship and rich ornamentation, the collector often made his choice on artistic grounds. In America, firearms were produced for a different class of people with more democratic and practical taste. While some arms, especially the "Golden Age" or the so called "Kentucky" rifle made by German-American gun-smiths may be lavishly ornamented, the vast majority are more interesting as historical objects than decorative pieces. Shoulder arms, primarily a product of modern age, are especially relevant to the development of the United States, and its place in world history.

Several types of rifles were used during the early part of the American Revolutionary time period. One of those in use was the Kentucky Rifle. These were usually made by German gun-makers in Maryland

and Pennsylvania. The French, 1763 Musket was also widely used by frontiersmen and Virginia long hunters. In addition, the British, "Brown Bess" rifle was one of the most renowned rifles ever produced and was one of the most significant firearms used during the American Revolution. The American Continental Army was armed with this weapon at the start of the war and as the war progressed; many more were manufactured by local gunsmiths. The rifle was used during the time of the Napoleonic Wars in Europe (1799-1815). It weighed a hefty 15 pounds with bayonet and fired a ball three quarters of an inch in diameter! However, it was not accurate over 60 yards.

KENTUCKY LONG RIFLE

The history of the United States is closely connected with the chronicle of the Kentucky Long Rifle. This old flintlock rifle is also known as the Kentucky Rifle, the Hog Rifle, or simply the Long Rifle. Slender and graceful, this rifle was the first truly American firearm which was created in the 1730's in Lancaster, Pennsylvania by skilled immigrant craftsmen from Germany and Switzer- land. The Kentucky Rifle reigned supreme for over a century as "state of art" until the coming of the "cap and ball" Percussion Rifle in 1840.

The rifles of the first American colonists were not rifles at all. They were smoothbore flintlock muskets imported from Europe. For a number of reasons, these old muskets were not suitable for the American frontier. First of all, they were so heavy that to go hunting with one was like carrying a fence rail on one's shoulders all day long. The Brown Bessie's, as these smoothbore muskets were called, fired spherical balls of lead and required large balls in order to get weight and striking force. They ranged from 0.60 to 0.70 inches in caliber, with corresponding hefty recoil when fired. They were therefore wasteful of powder and lead, both being scarce items on the American frontier. The large balls of the Bessie created other problems. They had high air-resistance, which slowed them greatly, giving them shorter range. Since the balls had no spin to balance the turbulence caused by slight surface imperfection, they curved wildly in flight, similar to a pitched "spitball" in a game of baseball. This erratic, unpredictable motion rendered these muskets ineffective beyond a range of about 60 yards.

The various defects were overcome by the Lancaster gunsmiths. First, they reduced the bores of the Kentucky Rifle to 0.45 to 0.50 calibers, so that one pound of lead, poured into iron molds, would produce from 70 to 120 spherical balls used for bullets, thus conserving valuable lead. The barrel length was increased to 40 inches, so as to get extra distance and impact from the expanding gunpowder. This greatly increased the range of the Kentucky Long Rifle compared to the Brown Bessie, which had a 30-inch barrel. Finally, the Kentucky Rifle was "rifled" with helical grooving in the barrel. This imparts rotary motion to the fired bullet on an axis that coincides with the line of flight (trajectory). This spin gives rifles greater range and accuracy, compared to smoothbores.

The Kentucky Long Rifle was more accurate than any previous firearm, and it soon became famous, far and wide, as being deadly at over 200 yards, which was an astounding range at that time.

This rifle became the primary weapon of the frontiersmen, especially in the remote and dangerous wilds of the frontier southwestern frontier. Although, it was used on the early frontier by the "Over Mountain Men", it was used extensively in Kentucky and led to the adoption of the name "Kentucky." Daniel Boone carried a Kentucky Rifle through the Cumberland Gap stopping at Martin's Station and spending several days with Captain Joseph Martin in 1775, who became the famous Cherokee Indian Agent, Virginia and North Carolina Militia Commander, the first General from Henry County, and finally a United States Representative from Colonial Virginia. He also held various other positions in the early days of the struggling new country of America.

Among the earliest documented working rifle makers are Adam Haymaker who had a thriving trade in the northern Shenandoah Valley of Virginia, and also the Moravian gun shops at both Christian Springs in Pennsylvania and also in the Salem area of central North Carolina. All three areas were busy and productive centers of rifle making by the 1750's. The Great Wagon Road was a bustling frontier thoroughfare, and traced this same route –

from eastern Pennsylvania, down the Shenandoah Valley, and spilling into both the Cumberland Gap into Kentucky and the Yadkin River (Salem) area of North Carolina. Rifle shops dotted the roads and kept the frontier supplied with the tools of exploration and conquest of the frontier.

The settlers of western Virginia, Tennessee, and North Carolina soon gained a reputation for hardy independence and rifle marksmanship as a way of life, further reinforced by the performance of rifleman in the American Revolution as well as the War of 1812. Through the war, the long rifles gained a more famous nickname of the Kentucky Rifle, coming from a popular song "The Hunters of Kentucky". This song was about Andrew Jackson and his victory at the Battle of New Orleans, where southern riflemen inflicted horrendous casualties to British invaders and suffered almost no losses themselves.

Just why the American rifle developed its characteristic long barrel is a matter of much conjecture. The German gunsmiths working in America would have been very familiar with German rifles, which seldom had barrels longer than 30 inches, and often had barrels much shorter. One good argument is that the gun could be loaded (from the muzzle) while on horseback, by resting the butt of the rifle on the ground. Another is that the longer barrel allowed for finer sighting and thus greater accuracy. But for whatever reason, by the 1750's it was common to see frontiersmen carrying a new and distinctive style of rifle that was used with great skill to provide tens of thousands of deer hides for the British leather industry.

These woodsmen were also exceptional trackers and Indian fighters, and played an important role in the French and Indian War which was in large part a guerilla war fought in many parts of the American back country. By the times of the American Revolution a strong tradition of rivalry had been ingrained into the citizens of Virginia, Pennsylvania, and North Carolina, and all lands west into the Indian territories.

Surprisingly, one of America's earliest triumphs in artistic and functional design, the "Kentucky Rifle," was not invented or generally fashioned in Kentucky. The name was coined from a hearty stock of American's who plied it.

Native Americans called Kentucky the "Dark and Bloody Ground" because of the unending wars between Iroquois and Cherokees for its possession. New worlders thought of the first Wild West as a hunter's paradise. In 1752, a stalwart American Indian trader named John Findley traveled the Ohio River documenting the valley's beauty and abundance. In 1769, a bold young explorer and skilled marksman, who was given an American-made flintlock rifle at the age of twelve, hired Findley and four other woodsmen to guide him through a wilderness country road between Kentucky and Tennessee which is now known as the "Cumberland Gap."

During the Revolution, demoralized English officers wrote home about a new type of American-made long-barreled "rifle" back woodsmen used with astonishing skill. When the war was won, the new government paid debts to its officers by offering land grants in untamed land. Claiming their acreage, these adventures brought their rifles to the new southwestern frontier.

Near the end of the War of 1812, American spirits were raised when five thousand Americans, including two-thousand frontiersmen with long barreled rifles, under the command of General Andrew Jackson, defeated the British in the Battle of New Orleans. A popular song called "The Hunters of Kentucky or The Battle of New Orleans" (no doubt, written by a proud Kentuckian) forever named America's Rifle.

"But Jackson, he was wide awake, and wasn't scared at trifles, for well he knew what aim we take, with our Kentucky Rifles."

Age, artistic beauty, and condition are the most important factors in gauging the value of the world's most sought-after firearm. A classic specimen is stocked in Native American tiger stripe maple. A rare colonial "Transition era (1715-1775)" flintlock specimen in a plain grain of maple, walnut, cherry, or birch, can command a huge sum. Keep in mind; most plain-wood Kentucky Rifles found today were during the third generation "percussion era. (1825-1860)"

A hinge door "patch-box" cut into the stock is the

distinguishing feature of a Kentucky Rifle. Most were made of brass and their decorative elements can often identify a gun's maker or geographic origin. Valuable "Golden age (1775-1825) Kentucky Rifles often have elaborate patch-boxes and carved stocks.

Like paintings, a rare signed work (the maker's name of initials on the barrel or elsewhere) of a great gunsmith artist is an important document of history. Most Kentucky Rifle makers, being humble Quakers, signed their work with their workmanship, not their name.

CHAPTER TEN

CHARACTERISTICS

Artistically, the long rifle is known for its often ornate decoration. The decorative arts of furniture making, painting, silver-smithing, gun- smithing, ect. All took their style cues from the prevailing trends of the day, and as in most things the fashion was set in Paris. Baroque and later rococo motifs found their way into all the decorative arts, and can be seen in the acanthus leaf scroll work so common on 18th century furniture and silver. The American frontier, as remote as it was, was not divorced from this trend, and the best American long rifles have art applied to them that is fully the equal of any Philadelphia cabinet or silver shop.

Originally rather plain, it didn't take long for the long rifle to be a source of pride for its owner, and by the 1770's every surface of the rifle could be used as a canvas for excellent applied art. Gunsmiths were recognized as the preeminent craftsmen of their day. It was the Gunsmiths job to be in top knowledge more than any other tradesmen of all materials used at the time. An accomplished gunsmith had to be a skilled blacksmith, whitesmith, wood carver, brass and silver founder, engraver, and wood finisher. While the European shops of the day had significant specialization of the trades leading to many separate tradesmen building each rifle, the frontier had no such luxury, and quite often only one gun maker, aided by perhaps a lone apprentice would make the entire rifle, a process almost unheard of in 18th century trade practice.

The long rifle is said by "modern experts" to have a range of 80 to 100 yards. However, in 1778 at the Siege of Boones borough, Kentucky one of the leaders of the combined British/ Shawnee assault force was hiding behind a tree. He stuck his head out from behind the tree and was instantly killed by a ball to the forehead fired by none other than the legendary Daniel Boone. This shot was later confirmed by witnesses on both sides and the distance measured at 250 yards. Hitting a target so precisely at that range would probably make the Kentucky Rifle comparable in total effective range with the British Maker rifle at 700 to 800 yards.

CHAPTER ELEVEN

DECLINE AND REBIRTH

By the turn of the 20th century, there was little traditional long rifle making left except in isolated pockets. The American long rifle, although well known and preserved in museums, was becoming an extinct species as far as modern workmanship was concerned. Few men were left who could build a long rifle. By the 1950's there was no one left in America who could make an entire rifle by hand, which involved forging the iron barrel from a flat bar, as well as forging all the parts for the gun lock and casting the brass parts in a small shop foundry. Popular interest in muzzle loading rifle shooting as a hobby spurred interest in the origins of the long rifle, and a few men began to search out the last remaining tradesmen who could shed some light on how the rifles were made.

CHAPTER TWELVE

BROWN BESS RIFLE

The Brown Bess was the principle weapon used by English troops during the colonization of Indian and American territories. The smooth bore, round barrel is made of polished steel. The butt plate, trigger guard assembly, ramrod ferrels and forend cap are highly polished brass. The lock and hammer are made of finely polished steel. The wood was generally European walnut with an oil finish. The 18th Century musket was essentially a smooth bore shotgun. After loading from the muzzle with loose black-powder and round lead bullet from a cylindrical, paper wrapped cartridge, their musket was fired by the flintlock action above the trigger. A rotating cock holding a piece of flint snapped forward to strike a pivoting L-shaped frizzen or "steel." That Action created sparks that ignited a small portion of priming powder in a projecting flash-pan sending flame through the barrels' touchhole to reach the main charge. Obviously, it would not perform well in rain and depended upon sharpened flit properly hardened steel for reliability.

The real problem, however, was the black powder quality. Following each firing, roughly 55 percent of the powder would remain as black sludge that built up inside the barrel clogging the touchhole and coating the lock. To cope with this clogging residue, the average ball was four to six hundreds of an inch smaller than bore size. Upon ignition, the undersized ball bounced and skidded up the barrel and proceeded in a direction determined by its last contact with the bore. Beyond 60 yards, the ball would lose its reliability to hit a man-sized target.

These limitations determined 18th century battle tactics, which employed long lines of men trained for speed of loading shooting rather than accuracy. They were expected to average volleys at enemy troops positioned 50-60 yards away. The typical battle was decided by a disciplined bayonet charge ending in a hand-to-hand melee.

To meet these combat conditions, the new British Brown Bess standard musket was designed to deliver a large bullet at low velocity. It employed a sturdy stock for use as a club in close fighting and had an overall length that combined with a long, socket bayonet to create a spear or pike for impacting an enemy's line. It was also designed to be durable and withstand the rigors of years of active campaigning. The Brown Bess successfully fulfilled all of these demands and more.

$\mathcal{C}$HAPTER $\mathcal{T}$HIRTEEN

PERCUSSION CAP

The percussion cap or primer was the crucial invention needed to make fire-arms that could fire in any weather. Before this development, firearms used igniters with flints or matched to set fire to a pan of gunpowder. A primer is a small disposable copper or brass cup, 4—6 mm in diameter (standard sizes are 0.175 inches and 0.210 inches for handgun and rifle cartridges). In the cup is a precise amount of stable but shock-sensitive explosive mixture, with ingredients such as lead azide or potassium perchlorate.

A striker hits the outside of the cup, which bends, and the explosive is crushed on an anvil. The shock-sensitive chemical compound explodes igniting a secondary charge of gunpowder or other explosive.

Caps were originally manually placed on nipples on the outside of single-shot muzzle-loading weapons. Pulling the trigger released a hammer to crush the cap against the nipple. Eventually, caps were incorporated into the rear of metallic cartridges. A small stamped anvil was added to the design, place inside the cup to make the modern replaceable primer.

Corrosive primers use stable, long lived explosives that generate corrosive residues in a gun, usually metallic oxides which, when exposed to moisture form hydroxides. They are popular with many militaries, because they work reliably under most severe conditions. Noncorrosive primers are somewhat less reliable when stored for many years, but far easier on guns. Most civilian ammunition use noncorrosive primers.

The invention that made the percussion cap possible was patented by the Reverend A. J. Forsyth in 1807. It consisted of priming with a fulminating power made of fulminate of mercury, chlorate of potash, sulphur, and charcoal, which was exploded by concussion. Joshua Shaw, an English born American immigrant is generally credited with the development of the first metallic percussion cap in 1814. Shaw's percussion caps used a mixture of fulminate of mercury, chlorate of potash, and ground glass contained in small metallic cup. This invention was gradually improved, and came to be used, first in the steel cap, and then in copper cap, by various gun makers and private individuals before coming into general military use nearly thirty years later.

The alteration of the military flintlock to the percussion musket was easily accomplished by replacing the powder pan with a perforated nipple. Replacing the cock or hammer, which held the flint by a smaller hammer formed with a hollow made to fit around the nipple when released by the trigger. On the nipple was placed the copper cap containing the detonating composition, now made of three parts of chlorate of potash, two of fulminate of mercury and one of powdered glass. The hollow in the hammer contained the fragments of the cap, if it fragmented, reducing the risk of injury to the firer's eyes.

The detonating cap, thus invented and adopted brought about the invention of modern cartridge case, and rendered possible the general adoption of the breech-loading principle for all varieties of rifles, shotguns and pistols.

CHAPTER FOURTEEN

THE GUNS THAT MADE AMERICA—1750–1892

American Revolution, Early Frontier Flintlock Muskets And Pistols

The flintlock muskets were the most important weapons in American history of the 18th Century. They provided the main means of hunting and defense for generations of settlers, hunters, farmers and adventures. Muskets were smooth-bored, single-shot, muzzle-loading simple weapons.

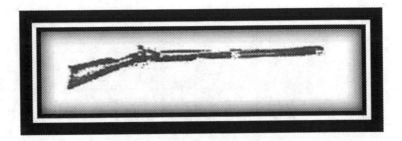

Kentucky Rifle
The Kentucky Rifle America's first great
contribution to firearm technology.

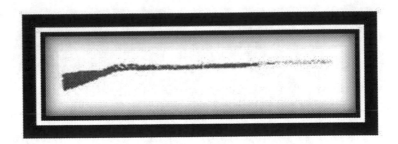

French "Charleville" Musket
The famous French Musket commonly referred to
as the "Charleville" Musket was used extensively
throughout the American Revolution.

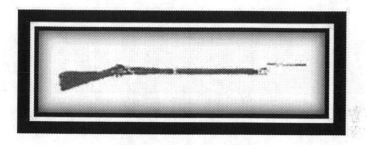

British "Brown Bess" Musket

The "Brown Bess" was the weapon used by the English troops during the colonization of India.

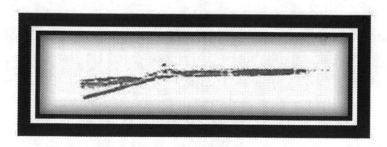

French 1763 Cavalry Carbine

Introduced during the American Revolution, this carbine offered light cavalry a short, light and versatile rifle.

Chapter Fifteen

WAGONS

The most common wagons used for hauling freight back East were the Conestoga's, developed in Penn Pennsylvania by descendants of German colonists.

Conestoga wagons were large, heavy, and had beds shaped somewhat like boats, with angled ends and a floor that sloped to the middle so barrels wouldn't roll out when the wagon was climbing or descending a hill. Like the covered wagons of the western pioneers, it had a watertight canvas bonnet to shelter the cargo. Conestoga's were pulled by teams of six to eight horses and could haul up to five tons.

Travelers on the Santa Fe Trail adopted the Conestoga design for its durability and size, but they found that bull-whackers or muleskinners were preferable to teamsters – the immense distances and scarcity of good water along the Santa Fe Trail precluded the use of horses as draft animals. Teams of up to two dozen oxen or mules were used to haul the heaviest loads. Sometimes a second wagon, or "back action," was hitched behind the lead wagon.

A. Prairie Schooner

Overlanders on the Oregon Trail, in contrast, quickly learned that Conestoga wagons were too big for their needs: the huge, heavy wagons killed even the sturdiest oxen before the journey was two-thirds complete. Their answer to the problem was dubbed the "Prairie Schooner, "a half-sized version of the Conestoga that typically measured 4 feet wide and 10 feet to 12 feet in length. With its tongue and neck yoke attached, its length doubled to about 23 feet. With the bonnet, a Prairie Schooner stood about 10 feet tall, and its wheelbase was over 5 feet wide. It weighed around 1300 pounds empty and could be easily dismantled for repairs en route. Teams of 4 to 6 oxen or 6 to 10 mules were sufficient to get the sturdy little wagons to Oregon.

Prairie schooner is a fanciful name for the covered wagon: the white canvas covers the wagons crossing the prairies and reminded some writers of the sails of a ship at sea. The covered wagon, also known as a *Prairie Schooner* is an icon of the American Old West.

Manufactured by the Studebaker brothers or any of a dozens of other wainwrights specializing in building wagons for the overland emigrants, a

Prairie Schooner in good repair offered shelter almost as good as a house. The wagon box, or bed, was made of hardwoods to resist shrinking in the dry air of the plains and deserts the emigrants had to cross. It was 2 feet to 3 feet deep, and with a bit of tar to seal the cracks and floor joints, it could easily be rendered watertight and floated across slow-moving rivers. The side boards were beveled outwards to keep rain from coming in under the edges of the bonnet and to help keep out river water. The box sat upon two sets of wheels of different sizes: the rear wheels were typically about 50" in diameter, while the front wheels were 44" in diameter. The smaller front wheels allowed for a little extra play, letting the wagon take slightly sharper turns than it would otherwise have been able to negotiate without necessitating a great deal of extra carpentry work to keep the bed level.

All four wheels had iron "tires" to protect the wooden rims, and they were likewise constructed of hard-woods to resist shrinkage. None-the- less, many emigrants took to soaking their wagon wheels in rivers and springs overnight, as it was not un-heard of for the dry air to shrink the wood so much that the iron tires would roll right off the wheels during the day.

Hardwood bows held up the heavy, brown bonnets. The bows were soaked until the wood became pliable, bending into U-shapes, and allowed to dry. They would hold their shape if this was done properly, which was important to the emigrants. If the wagon bows were under too much tension, they could spring loose and tear the bonnet while the wagon was jostled and jounced over rough terrain. The bonnets themselves were usually homespun cotton doubled over to make them watertight, hardly ever painted, as this stiffened the fabric and caused it to split. The bonnet was always well-secured against the wind, and its edges overlapped in back to keep out rain and dust. On some wagons, this is also angled outward at the front and back. As seen on previous page in the illustration, the bonnet can lend additional protection to the wagon's interior.

While wagons were minor marvels of Nineteenth Century engineering, they inevitably broke down or wore out from the difficulty and length of the journey. Equipment for making repairs en route was carried in a jockey box attached to one end or side of the wagon. It carried extra iron bolts, linch pins, skeins, nails, hoop iron, a variety of tools, and a jack. Also commonly found slung on the sides of emigrant wagons were water barrels, a butter churn, a shovel and axe, a tar bucket, a feed trough for the livestock, and a chicken coop. A fully outfitted wagon on the Oregon Trail must have been quite a sight, particularly with a coop full of clucking chickens raising a ruckus every time the wagon hit a rock.

There was only one set of springs on a Prairie Schooner, and they were underneath the rarely-used driver's seat. Without spring axles, riding inside a wagon was uncomfortable at the best of times. Some stretches of the Trail were so rough that an overlander could fill his butter churn with fresh milk in the morning, and the wagon would bounce around enough to churn a small lump of butter for the evening meal. The simple leaf springs under the driver's seat made that perch tenable, but not particularly comfortable. The brake lever was usually located so it could be pressed by the driver's foot or thrown by someone walking alongside the wagon, and it was ratcheted so the brake block would remain set against the wheel even after pressure was taken off the lever.

While Prairie Schooners were specifically built for overland travel, many emigrants instead braved the Oregon Trail in simple farm wagons retrofitted with bonnets. Farm wagons were typically slightly smaller than Prairie Schooners and not as well sheltered, as their bonnets usually were not cantilevered out at the front and back, but they were quite similar in most other respects.

Although covered wagons were commonly used for shorter moves within the United States, in the mid-nineteenth century thousands of Americans took them across the Great Plains to Oregon and California. Overland immigrants typically used farm wagons, fitting them with five or six wooden bows that arched from side to side across the wagon bed, then stretching canvas or some other sturdy cloth over the bows, creating the cylindrical cover.

Covered wagons were primarily used to transport goods. Small children, the elderly, and the sick or injured rode in them, but since the wagons had no suspension and the roads were rough, many people preferred to walk, unless they had horses to ride.

While covered wagons traveling short distances on good roads could be drawn by horses, those crossing the plains were usually drown by a team of two or more pairs of oxen. These were driven by a teamster or drover, who walked at the left side of the team and directed the oxen with verbal commands and whip cracks. Mules were also used; they were harnessed and driven by someone sitting in the wagon seat holding the reins.

One covered wagon generally represented five people. A well-to-do family might have two or three wagons, or a group of single men traveling together might share a wagon. While crossing the plains, emigrants banded together to form wagon trains for mutual assistance and occasionally defense. The covered wagons and wagon trains were retired late before the era of cars and planes.

B. Conestoga Wagon

The Conestoga wagon is a heavy, broad-wheeled covered wagon that was used extensively during the late 18th century and the 19th century in the United States and sometimes in Canada as well. It was large enough to transport loads up to 8 tons (7 metric tons), and was drawn by horses, mules or oxen. It was designed to resemble a boat, to help it cross rivers and streams, through it sometimes leaked unless one caulked the wagon.

The first Conestoga wagons originated in Pennsylvania sometime around 1750 and are thought to have been introduced by Mennonite German settlers. The name came from the Conestoga Valley Lancaster, Pennsylvania. In colonial times the Conestoga wagon was popular for migration southward through the Great Appalachian Valley along the distinguished Wagon Road. After the American Revolution it was used to open up commerce to Pittsburgh and Ohio. In 1820 rates charged were roughly one dollar per 100 pounds per 100 miles, with speeds about 15 miles (25 km) per day. The Conestoga, often in long wagon trains, was the primary overland cargo vehicle over the Appalachians until the development of the railroad. The wagon was pulled by a team of up to eight horses or up to a dozen oxen. For this purpose, the Conestoga horse, a special breed of medium to heavy draft horses, was developed.

The Conestoga wagon was cleverly built. Its floor curved upward to prevent the contents from tipping and shifting. The average Conestoga wagon was 18 feet long, 11 feet high, and 4 feet in width. It could carry up to 12,000 pounds of cargo. The cracks in the body of the wagon were stuffed with tar to protect them from leaking while crossing rivers. Also for protection against bad weather, stretched across the wagon was a tough, white canvas cover. The frame and suspension were made of wood, while the wheels were often iron-rimmed for greater durability. Water barrels built on the side of the wagon held water, and toolboxes held tools needed for repair on the wagon. The Conestoga wagon was used for many types of travel including passage to California during the California Gold Rush.

The term "Conestoga wagon" refers specifically to this type of vehicle; it is not a generic term for "covered wagon". The wagons used in the westward expansion of the United States were, for the most part, ordinary farm wagons fitted with canvas covers.

CHAPTER SIXTEEN

TRAVELLING IN A COVERED WAGON

The prairie schooner was one way that pioneers traveled. The prairie schooner was a large wagon with a large wagon with a framework over it. The frame was covered with white canvas. The wagons measured over a meter in width (four feet) and three and a half meters long (twelve feet) this wagon was a family's "home" for months.

In the wagon was everything that family would need – bedding, clothing, pots, pans and dishes, food and water, butter churns, washtubs, and pails. The pioneers also brought hunting gears along, such as plenty of guns and ammunition, topping the ride with needed furniture. Tools (crow-bar, axes, shovels, and hammer) and other supplies were hung on the sides of the wagon.

Clothing was packed in chests. Dishes, linens,

books, pictures and other special items were carefully packed in a trunk. The dishes used for the trip were made of tin.

Meals were prepared outdoors. Food that was packed for the long journey included bacon, coffee, flour, sugar, salt, corn meal, bags of rice, beans, and dried fruit. Water was carried in barrels.

Furniture for pioneers might include a table, chairs and spinning wheel. Furniture items not able to fit in the wagon, a person would have to buy or make by hand.

Cattle and chickens were also taken on the journey. The Cattle were tied to the wagon and walked along behind it. Chickens were kept in a coop.

CHAPTER SEVENTEEN

LIFE ON THE TRAIL

Pioneers often moved from one place to another by steamboat, flat boat, wagon (most often the Conestoga – a.k.a. Prairie Schooner), stagecoach, or by train. Sometimes they even came on foot, on mules or horseback.

With multiple choices of trails to take and places to go, many often took either the Santa Fe Trail to California or the Oregon Trail to the Oregon Territory. On the way they hunted for food. The early pioneers had plenty of game, but as more and more people came, good meat became less and less plentiful.

Pioneers moved because they were persuaded by the Homestead Act. They were adventuresome and ready for a new start.

Most pioneers moved by covered wagon. Most often, several wagons traveled together in a line called a Wagon Train. The wagons were small so, pioneers often stuffed in a much supplies as they could. They mostly brought food, dishes, and several pieces of special furniture for good use (as more could be made easily), clothing, bedding (quilts and pillows), farm animals, a weapon, and sometimes a small camping stove. Since the pioneers packed very heavily, sometimes they had to throw things out along the way. The wagons were for supplies, so people had to walk or ride horses next to the wagon.

There were no roads, just rough trails. People traveled together in wagon trains. This was safer and they could also help each other when necessary when the wagons broke down and needed to be repaired. Tools and supplies for repairing the wagons were kept in a box attached to the outside of the wagon.

Sometimes guides were hired to lead the wagon trains. A guide would know the shortest and safest route to take.

$\mathcal{C}$HAPTER $\mathcal{E}$IGHTEEN

SANTA FE TRAIL

The Santa Fe Trail was a significant historical and economical important commercial route from 1821 to 1880. The trail extended from the westernmost settlements of the United States in Missouri across the Plains Indian country to the New Mexico capital of Santa Fe. The date 1821 is generally accepted as the beginning of the Santa Fe Trail. In that year, Mexico established her independence from Spain and reversed Spanish policies of exclusiveness and resistances to foreign trade. For mutual protection the merchants commonly traveled in caravans with the mule or ox-drawn wagons arranged in two parallel lines so that they could be drawn into a circle quickly in case of attack. United States military escorts were furnished, but the soldiers were rarely needed, for the cautious plains Indians seldom risked battle with the well organized caravans.

The trail as originally traveled extended from Franklin or Independence, Missouri, westward past Council Grove to the Great Bend of the Arkansas, along the river almost to the Rocky Mountains before turning south over Raton Pass, (Pass of the Rat) to Santa Fe, New Mexico. There were, of course, several variants of the trail, but at least as early as 1825 the most popular route was the one known as the Cimarron Cutoff, which crossed the Arkansas River in western Kansas and proceeded in a more nearly southwestward direction to Lower Spring on the Cimarron River, up and across the Cimarron to the eastern New Mexican settlements and then to Santa Fe. After crossing the Arkansas River, this route lay entirely within territory claimed after 1836 by the Republic of Texas. In its later years the Santa Fe Trail became a link in the gold trail to California and in the immigrant trails to the far West.

CHAPTER NINETEEN

THE MARTIN HAMMACK STORY

Martin Hammack was born in 1791, 96th Military District, South Carolina near Greenville. His parents, Daniel and Mary "Polly" (Martin) Hammack, had settled in the old 96th Military District in the northwest part of South Carolina in what was Bounty Land given to Revolutionary War Veterans. They are shown in the 1790 census with a female infant and a female slave. Daniel and Mary were first cousins. Daniel was the son of John and Mary (Nellie) Martin Hammack. Daniel was sent to another family when his father died about 1770. During these hard times some children in families to poor to care for them were "bound out" or apprenticed for a trade with another family.

Shortly thereafter, the family moved, following the lead of Mary's older brother, Colonel William

Lucas Martin. After a stay of a few years, these families migrated west to what is now Smith County, Tennessee. Here in the wilderness, Colonel William Lucas Martin constructed a fort and three of his sisters, including Mary and a younger brother, Brice, settled. They probably migrated westward on the old Walton trail to the Hamlet of Dixon Springs on the border of Smith County and Trousdale County.

Daniel, according to the Smith County Archives at Cartage, Tennessee shows that he traded in properties, served on committees, juries and survey parties up until the time of his death in July, 16th 1829. His wife, Mary (Polly), died August 21, 1852. She was the daughter of General Joseph Martin and Sarah Lucas Martin.

Daniel and Mary (daughter of General Joseph Martin), are buried in the Colonel William Lucas Martin Cemetery north of Dixon Springs, Tennessee. The Colonel William L. Martin Cemetery was later called the Greer Cemetery. It was located on the Bellview Plantation of Colonel William Lucas Martin. In the southwest corner are two large, oblong sandstone boxes (crypts) covering the graves of Mary and Daniel. Some of Mary's other siblings are also buried here too. Inscriptions on the Daniel and Mary Hammacks headstones are still visible.

CHAPTER TWENTY

MILITARY SERVICE OF MARTIN HAMMACK

After growing to young manhood in Tennessee, at about 21 years of age, Martin Hammack enlisted in the United State Army for the War of 1812. His unit of Tennessee Militia was under the command of Major Brice Martin, who was his youngest Uncle and son of General Joseph Martin. The unit was under the command of General Andrew Jackson. The British about this time were stirring up the Indians in the southern states causing many early settlers to be killed. Martin Hammack served over a year before going home.

Before the battle of New Orleans took place, Martin Hammack enlisted in the Tennessee Mounted Gunmen under Captain Metcalf. This time his younger brother, Brice Hammack, went with him. The soldiers marched down the Natches Trace from

Nashville to the Mississippi and at New Orleans they fought the British in the Battle of New Orleans.

According to the Martin Hammack's military record, in 1816 he put in a claim for a horse he lost in action against the enemy. It does not say if he was reimbursed for his loss. Martin Hammack received his final discharge from the Army around the last of September, 1815. His pay was $8.00 a month plus $2.00 forage for his horse and $.40 a day for his own rations.

After returning home, he seemed to travel back and forth to Missouri, where he was a Wagon Master for trains going from Tennessee to the newly opened areas there. He and his brothers, Brice and William, settled in the new area.

It was at a Governor's Ball in St. Joseph where Martin met his future wife, Eleanor Ann McNair. She was living with her Uncle, Alexander McNair.

Alexander McNair was the first Governor of the State of Missouri. Eleanor was attending school at that time. The young couple married and moved north to Lincoln County, near her Father's home close to Troy, Missouri. Martin and Eleanor raised eight children in Lincoln County before migrating to California in April 1853.

CHAPTER TWENTY ONE

THE HAMMACK HOME IN MISSOURI

Martin Hammack and Eleanor Ann McNair were married January 9, 1822. They eloped. Their home for 31 years was a farm near New Hope, Lincoln County, Missouri. They had eight children: John, Brice, Mary, Martha, Margaret Ann, William, Robert and SaraThe Hammack Party headed west to California on April 15, 1853. The party arrived in Big Valley on April 14, 1854, where they made their home in Big Valley, Lakeport County, California.

During the early settling of the County, there were no hotels or other public places where travelers going through the County might remain overnight. The ranch house of Martin Hammack became a stopping place for many travelers. As far as it is known, no one was ever refused hospitality. On numerous occasions the children were required to give up their beds to strangers and travelers who would come to the ranch for the night. It was quite unusual for the family to partake of a meal without one or more strangers or travelers who were coming into the Valley for the location of land or for hunting and trapping purposes.

CHAPTER TWENTY TWO

HAMMACK FAMILY HISTORY

In the early 18th century many families migrated from Europe to America. Among the many families was John Hammack, a native of England who during early colonial period engaged in seafaring activities. As to what such activities were we do not know except that, based upon legend, one or more of the earlier Hammacks were active as pirates and buccaneers under Sir Henry Morgan. They participated in capturing and plundering of panama and Cuba in the late 17th Century.

The first member of the Hammack family who is known was John Hammack. He migrated to Virginia in colonial days and eventually made his home at what is now known as Greenville, South Carolina. John married a daughter, Mary (Nellie), of Captain Joseph Martin, Sr. who was an aristocratic pre-Revolution

Virginia family. After John's death, "Nellie" moved to Tennessee to be close to her Martin family.

When Martin Hammack was 18 years old and his brother John 16 years old, they became volunteers in the Army for the duration of the War of 1812 against England. They were in several engagements and fought in the Battle of New Orleans under the command of General Andrew Jackson. The battle was fought early in the morning of January 8, 1812. This happened several miles below the present city of New Orleans. From information handed down by them telling about the battle, it seems that everyone, including soldiers and civilians, were greatly excited and although the women in the area prepared food and were offering the soldiers gingerbread, cider and other edibles and drinks, most of the soldiers were too excited and nervous to enjoy them.

The old Revolutionary "Musket Rifle" which was nicknamed "Old Fremont" was originally owned by Major Brice Martin who had used it during the Revolutionary War and other frontier Indian wars. This same musket was used in the battle of New Orleans by another Major Brice Martin. In the later years, after it arrived in California, the musket became the property of Clara (Woods) rivers, a granddaughter of Martin Hammack.

In 2003, while doing family research in Missouri, Colonel Joe Martin (a relative of Martin Hammack) and his wife Linda found evidence that the rifle had traveled with the Martin Hammack's wagon train on a journey over the Santa Fe Trail to California in April 1853, after a winter layover to supply gold seekers with milk, butter and beef. After further research, it was found to be in the Lakeport Museum at Lake County, California in a storage room with other rifles, which none were being displayed at that time? After traveling to Lakeport the following January, it was determined this was indeed Major Brice Martin's rifle that had been taken on the Martin Hammack wagon train from Missouri to California in 1853. It was later passed down to Ms. Clara Woods Rivers, and she had given the rifle to the Museum in 1929. She was a descendant of Martin Hammack. Several Months after my visit to the Lake County Museum they authorized construction of a "Gun Room" and today "Old Fremont" the Revolutionary War Rifle, is on permanent display in its own glass display case in the museum.

The bayonet which was attached to the rifle and likewise used during both the Revolutionary War and the War of 1812 was passed down to Harold M. Hammack of Riverside, California. The whereabouts of the bayonet and this family is unknown.

Subsequent to the War of 1812, Martin Hammack became an Indian Scout traveling back and forth, from Tennessee to Missouri. He also fought in the Black Hawk Indian War of 1832. Martin Hammack's brother Brice Hammack became Judge of Lincoln County, Missouri.

Daniel Hammack, married General Joseph

Martin's daughter, Mary (Polly) Martin, they are the parents of Martin Hammack. Both are buried at Cato near Dixson Springs, Tennessee in Colonel Williams Lucas Cemetery.

CHAPTER TWENTY THREE

MCNAIR FAMILY HISTORY

Martin Hammack married Eleanor Ann McNair. The ancestral history which we have any knowledge of begins with her grandparents, Mr. and Mrs. John Crawford of Scotland. The Crawford's settled in North Ireland where a daughter, Margaret Ann was born. When she was 13 years old, the Crawford's immigrated to America and eventually settled in what is now Erie, Pennsylvania. Margaret Ann was in her teens when she married Robert McNair, who with his brother Alexander McNair, had fought in the Revolutionary War. Both were Lieutenants under General Marion, the "Swamp Fox", who was one of General George Washington's generals.

Robert McNair had a family of two daughters and four sons. The elder daughter, Eleanor Ann McNair, was born March 9, 1803. The other sister, whose name was Margaret Ann died while a young woman. The eldest son of Robert McNair was an Indian Scout joining and becoming a member of the Lewis and Clark Expedition and was killed by Indians. The other three McNair boys were drowned in the Mississippi River while engaged in a fight with Indians, upon the capsizing of the boat which they were in.

Alexander McNair came into the Territory of Missouri and later was the first Governor of the State of Missouri upon its attaining statehood. He married and had one daughter. The daughter having completed her schooling in St. Louis went by horseback from St. Louis to Philadelphia to finish her education. On one of the trips she met with an accident resulting in her death. Her cousin, Eleanor Ann, the elder daughter of Robert McNair, at the age of 16 years old, she moved to live with her Uncle, Alexander McNair in St. Louis. Her uncle desired to adopt her but Eleanor's father objected. She lived at Governor McNair's official mansion for about two years and while there attended a girls school. While living with her Uncle, Eleanor Ann McNair was quite active in society activities in the city of St. Louis and attended numerous state affairs with the Governor and his wife. It was at one of these affairs that Eleanor Ann met young Martin Hammack, an Indian Scout.

At the end of two years after living with Governor McNair the mother of Eleanor Ann became quite ill and she was required to return home, she being the eldest daughter of the family. The Robert McNair's lived in the town of St. Charles, Missouri. A few months after Eleanor returned to the home of her parents her mother died and Eleanor became her father's manager of the household.

Robert McNair at this time was engaged in the mercantile business. His business partner persuaded him to operate a boat on the Mississippi River and one night the boat and partner disappeared, leaving Robert McNair with no business, mercantile stock or other property, excepting his farm and a number of Negro slaves. During this early period of settlement in that part of the country along the Mississippi River, the Indians were a constant threat of danger. Quite frequently the settlers were required to take to the nearest Forts and remain there for weeks at a time while the Indians were on the warpath. After being notified by the Scouts, the gates of the Forts were sometimes required to be left open all night to enable the last of the settlers and their families to secure entrance to the Forts. During such times the settlers would move as much of their household goods and stock as they could take with them into the Forts.

Eleanor Ann McNair and Martin Hammack were married at St. Charles, Missouri, January 9, 1822. Robert McNair, her father objected to the marriage on the ground of the young age of his daughter. As a result, Eleanor Ann and Martin eloped. The young couple took up land near New Hope, Lincoln County, Missouri and engaged in farming for a period of approximately 31 years. To this union, eight children were born, namely: John, Brice, Mary, Martha, Margaret, Ann, William, Robert, Jasper, and Sarah Eleanor.

CHAPTER TWENTY FOUR

PREPARING FOR THE JOURNEY TO CALIFORNIA

Brice Martin Hammack, the son of Martin Hammack, was a 49er, going to California in the early part of 1849, where he remained for two years. He was so taken with the west that he decided to return to Missouri, marry the girl he had left there, and return to California to make his permanent home. While in California he personally recovered sufficient gold to have a ring made for each of his sisters. The rings were made in Sacramento before he returned to his home in Missouri. In addition to the rings he had made for his sisters, he had another ring made for his intended wife, Elizabeth Ann Gray.

Upon the knowledge of the prospective return from California of Brice, his parents, the Martin Hammacks, prepared a great feast for his homecoming. There was a barbecued beef, and other meats, wild game, gingerbread, a barrel of cider and plenty of other hard liquor. All their relatives and friends came to the homecoming celebration to hear of his journey to the gold state. His journey to California was over the northern route along the Oregon Trail, and the return trip was made by boat from San Francisco to Panama, then across Panama and finally a boat to New Orleans, and then up the Mississippi River to St. Charles, Missouri.

Brice Hammack and Elizabeth Grey were married at her home in Lincoln County, Missouri, on Christmas Day, 1852. Elizabeth was one of a large family of children. Her mother having died, Elizabeth had to take the place of the mother and care for the other children. Her father being in a bad financial condition, all the children were required to do such work as they could perform and find, to help with the support of the large family.

Martin Hammack and his wife Eleanor, having decided they could not experience their son Brice going back to California to make his home and the probability of never returning, they decided to sell their properties and take all their children and go with Brice and his new wife to California to establish new homes. The preparation for the overland trip required much planning and would take over six months.

Martin Hammack made a trip to St. Louis and specially ordered thirteen overland wagons to be constructed for the long and rough journey to

California. He had the wagons constructed with two floors or compartments. All the provisions were to be stored on the lower floor, and all household goods occupying the upper floor. These wagons were the typical prairie schooner with bows, covered with heavy canvas tarpaulin, which were oiled to make them waterproof. The wagons were all painted black with the exception of one, which was painted a red color to distinguish their wagon train on the overland journey. At this time the vast prairies and desert areas were lined with emigrants going west, most of the emigrants being gold seekers traveling to California to make their fortunes. In connection with the overland emigrants the statement has been made that, "the weak died on the way and the cowards never started".

During several months that preparations were being made for the journey to California, Martin Hammack returned to his relatives home in Tennessee, to bid them farewell and to obtain several rifles to be taken along on the overland trip. Martin Hammack having been an Indian Scout well knew the ways of the Indians, who were dangerous and very treacherous in those times. When he made another trip to St. Louis to obtain the wagons he purchased a large supply of provisions and ammunition for the trip. Martin Hammack also purchased a plentiful supply of colored beads, cheap jewelry, and other trinkets to be used as a peace offering to the Indians and for trading purposes.

One of the old flintlock rifles Martin Hammack's ancestor had used during the Revolution was one of the rifles he obtained in Tennessee for his overland journey to California. As stated, it was passed down to a Granddaughter, Clara Woods Rivers, and is now on display at the Lake County Museum, together with a set of candle molds which were brought from the old home in Missouri and a chair that belonged to the Martin Hammack family. Homemade candles at the time of the journey were the only lights used, even oil lamps were then unknown.

The Lincoln County, Missouri farm of Martin Hammack was sold to a cousin and at the time of the sale, there was a three day sale of livestock, farm machinery and household furniture, all of which were very crude at that time. The beds generally in use were known as trundle beds. Attached to them being a smaller bed underneath and pushed back under the larger bed when not in use. A general sale in those days was an unusual and exciting event. In connection with the sale of Martin's property and goods, several days were spent in preparing the food to be provided to everyone. They had long tables out under the trees in the yard near the house where lunches were served. The people came with their families in wagons principally drawn by oxen which were the primary mode of travel in those days. The man who purchased the furniture handed to Martin Hammack's wife a chair and told her to use it for herself on the overland journey.

CHAPTER TWENTY FIVE

DEPARTING ON THE CALIFORNIA JOURNEY

Margaret Ann Hammack and Woods Crawford were married October 13, 1852. They drove one of Martin Hammack's wagons on the overland trip and Brice Hammack and his bride drove another wagon. Martin Hammack and his wife and younger children used another wagon and the other ones held their goods and equipment. Robert Hammack drove the family wagon as his father, Martin Hammack, being the wagon master and head of the overland wagon party, always rode horse back in advance of the wagon train.

The Hammack party departed from new Hope, Missouri, in the early morning of April 15, 1853, for their journey to California. After starting, but before leaving the State of Missouri, sickness was experienced by some of the younger children, resulting in the entire party being delayed a month. The wagon train crossed the plains by way of the Santa Fe Trail and nearly six months passed before completing the journey. They drove oxen and were required to travel very slowly as there were no roads. Other wagon trains using horses passed them by and the younger members of the party would become quite discouraged. However, after a few days the slow, steady oxen overtook the horse trains which would be laid up by the side of the trails or roads being followed. The horses could not endure the hardships of overland traveling to the extent that the oxen could.

Martin Hammack, being the wagon master of the wagon train, always selected the camp site where they could have feed and water for their stock. Every night the men of the party took their turns as guards for the camp. They had a herd of dairy cattle with them in addition to the oxen and horses. When butter was needed a churn of cream was suspended beneath one of the wagons to churn and by nightfall they had butter.

During the journey one of Martin Hammack's blooded saddle horses was stolen by the Indians. Some of the men in the party tracked the stolen horse to an Indian camp but were afraid to make a demand on the Indians for the horse. Some of the cattle also were stolen at different times along the journey. When camp was made, all the wagons were drawn up in a circle and no lights or fires were allowed in the camp after dark due to the danger of Indian attacks. All slept in the wagons with the tarpaulin covers drawn close, as the Indians frequently shot arrows at the wagons during the night. The men who stood guard at night were furnished with heavy tarpaulin covers as it was often stormy and cold.

On one occasion, Martin Hammack rode ahead of the wagon train and became lost in making an escape from Indians. He was out all night and no one slept during that night thinking that surly the Indians had either killed or captured him. The wagon train party had a large conch shell which was used when any member of the party became lost, the sound of this carried for many miles, particularly during the stillness of the night. It was blown throughout the night and although he could hear it, the wind was so strong he could not locate the direction of the sound. With the arrival of morning the wind died down and he was able to determine the direction of the sound and made it back to the wagon train in due time.

Martin Hammack had leaned the Indian Language while working as an Indian Scout. Many times during the journey an Indian Chief would come to the wagon train to hold conversation with him. He always treated them with consideration and respect and gave them trinkets, which always pleased the Indians. The Chiefs were usually large, straight, fine looking men, wearing their hair long, with copper bands around their arms and large colored earrings. The Indians made fine moccasins of buckskin, which they traded for beads and other small trinkets. They had not as yet learned the value of money so they had no use for it. At one time Martin tried to purchase a pony from an Indian, offering him a $20.00 gold piece, but the Indian would not accept it stating he wanted that many dollars and not in one gold piece.

There were crude ferries across some of the rivers which had to be traversed during the journey and other rivers had to be ferried across in their wagon beds. In cases of wide or swift rivers this kind of ferrying across was quite an undertaking as the wagons had to be taken apart and all the provisions removed from the lower floor. The livestock had to swim across and some of them were lost by drowning.

There were trading posts along the route and members of the wagon train always looked forward to a treat when they came to any of these trading posts. At these post provisions and ammunition were replenished, which were very expensive. The members of the party were seldom, if ever without fresh meat as there were all kinds of wild game to be had. Buffaloes were seen by the thousands along different parts of the overland route, but except in the case of young buffaloes the meat was coarse and very dark, although today buffalo meat is widely accepted as good tasting and is plentiful in some areas of the country.

During the journey a cousin and one other member of the party died on the plains. The bodies were carried in the wagon all the next day and buried after dark. This was to keep the Indians from discovering or disturbing the bodies. The top of the grave was filled and covered with rocks to prevent the coyotes and other animals from disturbing the grave.

There were a number of dogs taken along the trip. Their feet would become very sore from the rough travel. To eliminate this, Martin Hammack's wife and other women of the party made buckskin boots for the dogs which were fitted on their feet and proved to be of great benefit to them. They appeared to be thankful.

$\mathcal{C}$HAPTER $\mathcal{T}$WENTY $\mathcal{S}$IX

SHASTA CITY, CALIFORNIA

After six months of hard and dangerous travel, the party reached Shasta City, California late in the fall of 1853. It was there they decided to spend the winter in a mining camp named Middletown, located not far from Shasta City. During that winter, some of the men prospected for gold while others hauled freight with the oxen teams from Shasta City by way of Colusa to Marysville, then onto Yuba City. Milk was sold from the dairy cattle to miners for 25 cents a quart. During this winter, a provisions man gave Sarah Hammack, who was a child of only eight years old, a can of California peaches, which was the first they had ever seen or eaten.

It was during the winter in the mining Camp at Middletown that the members of the Hammack party first met Jonas Ingram. At that time he was recovering from a siege of pneumonia and not being able to work spent considerable time in the camp. During these visits he became acquainted with one of the Hammack daughters and resulting from such acquaintance he later went on to Lake County, making the trip on horseback.

CHAPTER TWENTY SEVEN

COLUSA, CALIFORNIA

The Hammack party left Shasta City during the early spring of 1854 and traveled south as far as Colusa and there made camp on the banks of the Sacramento River, while searching for land suitable for ranching. It was at that time that Martin Hammack received reports from certain hunters and trappers who came into the camp, telling him of a beautiful lake and valley some distance to the west. Resulting from the reports he had two of the members of the party to make an exploratory trip into what is now Lake County, and they returned after several weeks and verified the reports as to the beautiful lake and country surrounding what is now known today as Clear Lake. They reported a wonderful body of fresh water plentiful with fish, game in the valleys and mountains and that the wild oats were growing four to five feet high.

CHAPTER TWENTY EIGHT

ARRIVAL IN LAKE COUNTY

With that report Martin Hammack decided to travel on to the new territory as it was just what the members of the party were searching for. The party started at once for the Lake, it then being a beautiful wild country with plenty of feed for stock and wild game of all kinds of meat. It was a common sight to see herds of deer resting in the shade of the oak trees of Big Valley, which was then almost wholly covered with large oak trees, and certainly a land of plenty. At that time, Big Valley was inhabited almost entirely by Indians. Although, a few white hunters and trappers had drifted into the Valley, none of them had made any permanent homes in either Big Valley or any other part of Lake County.

About the year 1840, a Spaniard by the name of Salvador de Vallejo, a brother of the famous Spanish Governor Vallejo, came into Big Valley with a large herd of cattle. Salvador de Vallejo constructed a stone house and stock corrals just north of the present town of Kelseyville. In 1847 he sold his cattle to two men by the names of Stone and Kelsey. These men erected an adobe house and employed Indians to work for them. For a while all went well and the Indians remained satisfied with their working conditions. The Indian men acted as Vaqueros and the Indian women doing the house work, gathering the wood and other menial labor. As time passed, Stone and Kelsey so worked the Indians and mistreated them as to practically make them slaves. As a result, the Indians decided to rise up against them in revenge. The Indians had their squaws steal the white men's guns and fill them with sand and mud so that they could not be used.

The attack on Stone and Kelsey was made by the Indians during the early morning and before Stone and Kelsey had left their cabin. The Indians had banded together in quite a number, some coming from a long distance. As a result of the Indians attack both Stone and Kelsey were killed and a number of other persons severely wounded and injured. During the attack, one of the Indians, still friendly to Stone and Kelsey, slipped away and by the trail rode to Sonoma County and gave the alarm to the Government officials. The Government sent soldiers into Lake County but when they arrived, Stone and Kelsey had been killed and the adobe house was burned and destroyed. By reason of the attack, the Government soldiers with their cannon fire gave the Indians such fright, many of them ran for a considerable distance and some were even driven into the Lake and drowned. The Government soldiers had such a difficult time in moving the Cannon over the mountains between Sonoma and Lake Counties, there being no roads of any king, they decided to abandon the cannons and not return them to Sonoma. In order to prevent the Indians from taking the Cannons they were sunk in the Lake.

At the time of the arrival of the Hammack party in Big Valley in April, 1854, the only white people in the County were a few hunters and trappers, probably not more than six in number who were unmarried and had no families except that some of them had Indian women living with them. Among those who were then in Lake County was Robert Gaddy. In 1853, he had erected a log cabin near where the town of Lower Lake is now located. Another cabin was erected by Broone, Smith and Graves who were survivors of the Donner party. Their cabin was located near the base of Mt. Knocti at the eastern edge of Big Valley.

The Hammack party, led by Martin and Brice Hammack and consisting of twenty-five persons, came into Lake County during the month of April, 1854, and it is the generally accepted historical fact that such party constituted the first white settlers in Lake County. The actual date of the arrival in Big Valley was April 14, 1854, and the first camp site of the Hammack party in Big Valley was where the town of Kelseyville is now located at the upper end of the Valley and on the west bank of Kelsey Creek, and near the burned and destroyed adobe house of Stone and Kelsey, where their massacre by the Indians occurred.

The route of travel used by the Hammack party in coming into Lake County was by way of the present city of Napa, California; Yountville and over Howell Mountain, into Polk Valley. Then over Polk Mountain and the Coyote valley, the present site of the town of Lower Lake. From there over Seiglar Mountain and the sand hills into Big Valley. Extreme difficulties were experienced in traveling over the mountains as there were no roads or trails. Many times it was necessary to rope trees to the back of wagons to prevent them from running over the oxen teams. In traveling down the sand hills above Kelseyville it was necessary to use ropes to prevent the wagons from slipping down the steep hills and turning over. There were four yoke of oxen to each wagon, which were the first wagons brought into the County with families or by any person except those used by the soldiers at the time the expedition came into Lake County after the massacre of Stone and Kelsey.

Shortly after the first camp was established on the west side of Kelsey Creek, the camp being formed by the wagons and tents being placed in a circle around a large oak tree, a large California bear entered the camp one night and created quite a noise and commotion among the kettles and kitchen utensils which were stacked about the base of a large tree.

The camp being formed in a circle it was realized it would be dangerous to attempt to shoot the bear while in the middle of the camp, so the bear was run out of the camp by the dogs and then shot by some of the men.

Not long after the arrival of the Hammack party, Martin, Brice and Woods Crawford and some of the other members of the party made their locations of homesteads, which were located in the lower part of the Valley bordering and above the south shore of Clear Lake. After the homestead locations were made, the members of the party commenced securing materials for the houses and other buildings. They traveled to Seiglar Mountain and split out cedar planks and boards which were shaved and smoothed by hand with broad axes. These planks were about six feet in length and including the studding, were all hewn and smoothed by hand. As soon as the materials were acquired, work commenced on the homes in the several homestead locations. The fireplace stones were taken from the burned adobe house of Stone and Kelsey, and such nails as were used were very crude.

During this early period all cooking was done over the fireplaces with iron kettles used for boiling food and water. Dutch ovens were used for all baking. At different times there was no flour available and the party had to use boiled wheat. When they were out of coffee, the water from the boiled wheat was used as a substitute for coffee. The wheat raised in the Valley was transported on horseback to Napa County to be ground into flour and a week's time was required to make the journey, there being no roads but only rough trail.

The first house constructed by any member of the party was the Woods Crawford house erected about one-half mile above the south shore of Clear Lake and near where the present Big Valley Indian Rancheria is located. The home of Brice Hammack was stationed and erected about one-half mile from the south side of Clear Lake and on property which later became known as the Boardman Ranch.

The Martin Hammack ranch included what is now known as the Hurlbert and Mills ranches located about one mile above the Lake shore and between Kelsey Creek and McGaugh Slough. The original ranch house remained in place for a number of years and part of it still in existence in 1939. Martin and Brice Hammack had brought into the Valley some two hundred head of find stock consisting of horses, oxen and dairy cattle.

At the time of the original settlement in Big Valley wild game consisting of bear, elk, deer and other smaller animals were plentiful. The bear were principally the California brown bear, with a few grizzlies, and the bears were considered more dangerous than the Indians. At different times bear traps consisting of logs erected near what is now known as Highland Springs, and it was great sport to engage in that pastime. The bear meat was not desirable as a food and the Indians would not even touch it, they considering bear meat as a food of the Devil. Moreover, the Indians, after the killing of Stone and Kelsey, had a great choice of beef in addition to all the wild game and fish to be had.

Until May 20, 1861, during the time of the original settlement of Big Valley and Lake County the territory which is now embraced within Lake County constituted a part of Napa County. On November 6, 1855, Clear Lake Township, as a part of Napa County, was organized, and Lake County as a separate county was created under date of May 20, 1861, and at that time the first county election held. The first court house in the County was erected at Lakeport and destroyed by fire during the night of February 16, 1867. The court house was then removed to Lower Lake and after a long struggle was finally returned to Lakeport where it has since remained.

During the first few years after beginning of settlement of the County all supplies were obtained in the City of Napa and transported by pack horses over a narrow mountain trail. The first store erected and operated in Lake County was that owned by a Dr. E.B. Boynton at what is now known as Rocky Point on the Shore of Clear Lake north of Lakeport. Later his store was moved to the knoll south of Lakeport, which has been known for some years as the Bleakmore place.

In 1858, Mr. A. Levy became the owner and operator of said store. Mr. A. Levy first traveled into Lake County as a wandering Jewish peddler with a pack of dry goods on his back. Throughout the remaining years of Mr. Levy's life he always remembered the first night spent by him in the Big Valley was at the ranch home of Martin Hammack. Mr. Levy's next trip into the County was made with a pack mule and as his business increased, a pack team was employed and later by wagon train.

Shortly after Clear Lake Township was established the first school house in the County was erected consisting of a rough pine board one-room building. The school house was located east of McGaugh's Slough near the ranch of Thomas "Dobe" Boyd and was known in later years as the Rickabaugh ranch.

The first church organized in the County was the Methodist Church South in 1857 and the school house for some time was used for church purposes. The First Baptist Church was organized in the spring of 1861. Martin Hammack, his daughter Sarah and two granddaughters united with this church and were baptized in Adobe Creek on the Brice Hammack ranch. The records of this church were destroyed when the first court house was burned in 1867. Martin Hammack's wife had, from a small child, been a member of the Scotch Presbyterian Church although later attended the Baptist Church after it was organized in Lake County. From those who knew her after settling in Lake County she was known as a woman of great character and fortitude, never complaining of the many hardships that had to b endured as at all times traveling and assisting the sick and other persons throughout the County requiring aid and assistance. All of her traveling was done by horseback, sometimes requiring two or three days or even weeks on some of her mercy trips. She also was known as a great friend of the Indians, providing food and clothing for them and after an orchard and garden had been brought into production on the ranch the Indians was never refused their requests for vegetables and fruit. It was a common saying by the Indians that "all Indians like old lady—heap good to Indians."

During the early settling of the County there were no hotels or other public places where travelers through the County might remain overnight. Almost universally all persons traveling through Big Valley remained at the ranch house of Martin Hammack and so far as known no one was ever refused hospitality. On numerous occasions the children were required to give up their beds to strangers and travelers who would come to the ranch for remaining overnight. It was quite unusual for the family to partake of a meal without one or more strangers or travelers who were coming into the Valley for the location of land or for hunting and trapping purposes. A certain Preacher by the name of Davis, and his wife, remained one entire winter at the Martin Hammack ranch. The preacher wore white shirts and his wife would iron them on the top of an old green trunk which

Martin had brought all the way from his old home in Missouri.

Near the Martin Hammack ranch house, an Indian trail passed, extending from the upper end of Big Valley down to the Lake shore near the mouth of McGaugh Slough. This trail was used almost daily by the Indians going to the Lake for hunting and fishing. They always traveled in single file and many times the squaws would be carrying large baskets of wood. These baskets were made of willow and lake tulles and were strapped to the shoulders of the Indian women. During the fall period the women would gather acorns, which were ground between stones and used for flour to make bread.

Sometime after the Woods Crawford family had taken up their homestead in the Valley, Woods became active in politics, first being Justice of the Peace of Clear Lake Township and in later years serving two terms as District Attorney of Lake County. He is credited with giving the town of Lakeport its name. Upon the death of Woods Crawford his son, Colonel Crockett Crawford, took over his father's law practice, later serving as District Attorney for two terms, of Lake County and upon Colonel Crawford's retirement from active law practice his son Howard Crawford assumed such practice and in 1939 was conducting the same in Lakeport.

Brice Martin Hammack was born January 23, 1825. Elizabeth Ann Grey was born March 8, 1831. They were married at the home of her father in Lincol

County, Missouri, on Christmas day, 1852. To this union four children were born in Big Valley, Lake County, California. The names and dates of birth of those children are as follows: Sarah Eleanor, May 31, 1854; Martha Anna, November 23, 1856; Henry Martin, January 5, 1859; and George W., December 15, 1864. Of this family, only Martha Ann and Henry Martin Hammack survived to this date, 1939. Sarah Eleanor Hammack was the first white child born in Lake County. Although, it has been considered by some that George Reeves, son of Elijah Reeves, who was the first white child born in Lake County, yet that does not seem possible when it is considered that Elijah Reeves family did not arrive in Lake County until some considerable time following the arrival of the Hammack party on April 14, 1854. The birth of Sarah Eleanor Hammack occurred May 31, 1854, approximately six weeks subsequent to the arrival of the Hammack party in Big Valley.

Jonas Ingram was born in Jackson County, Illinois, April 17, 1823. Martha Susan Hammack was born in New Hope Missouri, April 17, 1835. Jonas Ingram had first met the members of the Hammack party during the winter of 1853-1854 while that party was temporarily living at the town of Middleton, Shasta County, California. Jonas Ingram had come to California in 1849 following the discovery of gold, and was engaged in prospecting and mining up to the time of his going to Lake County in 1854. He took a strong fancy to Martha Susan Hammack so he decided to go the Clear Lake Valley with the hope of finding the Hammack party. He arrived in Big Valley in April 1854, and within a few weeks asked to marry the daughter, Martha Susan Hammack.

In June of 1854 Martin Hammack and his daughter Martha, with Jonas Ingram, traveled by horseback over the mountain trail to Napa City for the marriage of Jonas and Martha. In the saddlebags she carried her wedding gown that she and her mother had made by hand, ever stitch being extremely small and perfectly set. Jonas Ingram carried in his pocket the wedding ring that he had made from a gold nugget found in the mines of Shasta County. The wedding trip required two days each way, being made on horseback, there being only a rough trail to be followed. The wedding was the first wedding originating in Lake County and Martha Susan Hammack was the first bride from Lake County. To this union ten children were born, as follows: Charles Leroy, July 10, 1856; Elizabeth, September 9, 1858; Henry, September 24, 1860; Mary Ellen, November 9, 1862; Susan, April 7, 1865; Margaret Francis, February 12, 1867; Sarah, June 2, 1869; Belle, October 19, 1871; Martha, February 28, 1873; Baby Ingram, November 8, 1876. Of this large family, only Elizabeth, Mary Ellen and Belle survive to this date, 1939.

Woods Crawford was born in Richland County, Ohio, December 8, 1829, and he and Margaret Ann Hammack were married October 13, 1852, at the home of her parents in New Hope, Lincoln Cour

Missouri. To this union seven children were born, as follows: Florence H., Crockett M., Susan R., Mary L., Elizabeth, Emma P., and Frank. Crockett Crawford, known as the Colonel Crawford, was the second white child born in Lake County. After retiring, Colonel Crawford remained in Lake County the remainder of his life and was still living in 1939.

E.B. Bole was born in Morgan County, Ohio, June 12, 1825. Mary Jane Hammack was born in New Hope, Lincoln County, Missouri. They were married August 22, 1858, and to this union six children were born as follows: Albert G., Harriett A., Mary Ellen, Francis A., Willie and Martha J. Four sisters survive this family, Amanda, Mary Ellen, Annie and Martha in 1939.

Another member of the Hammack family, namely John Hammack, was a school teacher in Lake County for several years and then returned to the State of Missouri where he married, and, while still a young man, passed away.

Of the other original members of the Hammack party William and Robert Hammack never were married, and, after engaging in different activities in Lake County for a number of years, passed away in Lake County, both having lived many years.

William Monroe Woods was born in Greenville, North Carolina. Sarah Eleanor Hammack was born March 30, 1845, in Elsberry, Lincoln County, Missouri. They married in Ukiah, Mendocino Country,

California, in December, 1881, and of this union three children were born:

1. Clara Eleanor, January 27, 1884
2. Jessie, July 4, 1885
3. James Monroe, December 22, 1887

Clara Eleanor and James Monroe survived past 1939.

Martin Hammack passed away in Big Valley, Lake County, California on August 31, 1873, at the age of 84 years. His wife, Eleanor Ann passed away at the home of her daughter, Sarah Woods, in Lakeport, California, February 14, 1888, at the age of 86 years.

Colonel William Monroe Woods passed away at his home in Lakeport, California, May 13, 1891, at the age of 65 years. Sarah Eleanor, his wife, passed away at her home in Lakeport, January 15, 1923, at the age of 75 years.

CHAPTER TWENTY NINE

PICTURES OF HAMMACK FAMILY MEMBERS

Lakeport, California

Martin Hammack & Eleanor McNair Hammack
(Right side)

William (Will) Hammack, Son of Martin
Hammack & Eleanor McNair Hammack
(Left side)

Sara Ellen Hammack and Peter Bean
Sara Ellen Hammack was wife of Peter Bean.
Daughter of Brice Hammack &
Eleanor McNair Hammack.
She was born on May 31, 1854 being the
first white child born in Lake County.
Peter Bean's picture was taken around 1897.

Elizabeth Ann Grey Hammack(Wife
of Brice Martin Hammack)

Valentine Hammack (Far Left)
Frank Clair Hammack (Middle)
George Herbert Hammack (Far Right)

George's parents home near Finley, California.
In the picture is his mother and children:
Standing are Mae & Herbert,
Sitting are Valentine, Frank & Merle.

The George Washington Hammack Family

George Washington Hammack to the left.
Brice & Mary Elizabeth Hammack on the right.

*George Washington Hammack was
the son of Brice Martin
Hammack and Elizabeth Ann Gray. He was born on
December 15, 1864 and died on January 7, 1933.
He married Minnie Jane Spect. She was born on
October 2, 1867 and died on February 24, 1907.
From this marriage there were seven children:
Brice Levi, Harry, Harold Merle, Frank Clair,
Valentine, George Herbert and Mary Elizabeth.*

George Washington Hammack
(Son of Brice Hammack & Elizabeth
Ann Gray Hammack)

Elizabeth Ann Gray Hammack with
George Hammack's children:
Standing – Mae Hammack Cross,
& Herbert Hammack,
Sitting in front – Valentine, Clair & Merle Hammack

Henry Martin Hammack

Henry Martin   November 1937   Buddy's parent's home
Henry Martin was known to most as Buddy.
He was the son of Brice Martin Hammack
and Elizabeth Ann Gray Hammack. He
was born on January 5, 1859 and died on
April 6, 1943. In his later years he became
the caretaker at the Reeves Ranch.

Buddy and Max Meadows   Clair Hammack

Jim Woods & Clara Woods
Children of Sara Eleanor Hammack
& William Monroe Woods

Clara Woods
Daughter of Sara Eleanor
Hammack & William Monroe Woods

Ebanezer Buckingham Bole
Husband of Mary Jane Hammack who
is the daughter of Martin Hammack &
Eleanor Ann McNair Hammack

Mary Jane Hammack
Wife of Ebanezer Buckingham Bole
& daughter of Martin Hammack &
Eleanor Ann McNair Hammack.

John Smith Eakle
Husband of Martha Anna Hammack

Martha Anna Hammack
Wife of John Smith Eakle
Daughter of Brice & Eleanor McNair Hammack

1884   Martha J. Bole   1886
(Unknown Hammack)
Martha J. Bole is the daughter of Mary
Jane Hammack (daughter of Martin &
Eleanor Hammack) and Ebenezer Bole.

Ingrams
Possibly Jonas Ingram & Susan Hammack

Mary Jane Hammack
Daughter of Martin Hammack &
Eleanor Ann McNair Hammack
Married Ebanezer Buckingham

CHAPTER THIRTY

FAMILY RELATIONSHIP

* Daniel Hammack was a son of Mary "Nellie" Martin Hammack and John Hammack, General Joseph Martin's sister.

* Daniel Hammack married his cousin, Marry "Polly" Martin, daughter of General Joseph Martin.

* Martin Hammack was the son of Daniel Hammack and Mary "Polly" Martin.

Descendants of Daniel Hammack

Generation No. 1

1. DANIEL[1] HAMMACK He married MARY (POLLY) MARTIN.

Child of DANIEL1 HAMMACK and MARY MARTIN is:

2. i. MARTIN[2] HAMMACK, b. 1791, 96th District, Greenville, South Carolina; d. 31 August 1873, Big Valley, Lake County, California.

Generation No. 2

2. MARTIN[2] HAMMACK (DANIEL[1]) was born 1791 in 96th District, Greenville, South Carolina, and died 31 August 1873 in Big Valley, Lake County, California. He married ELEANOR ANN McNAIR 09 January 1822 in St. Charles, St. Charles County, Missouri, daughter of ROBERT McNAIR and MARGARET CRAWFORD. She was born 09 March 1803 in Pennsylvania, and died 14 February 1888 in Lakeport, California.

Notes for MARTIN HAMMACK
Martin lived in South Carolina, Tennessee, Missouri, California and Georgia.
Church Affiliation was Baptist

Military Service: Black Hawk War of 1810
Occupation: Farmer:
More about MARTIN HAMMACK:
Burial: August 1873, Hartley Cemetery, Lakeport, California

Notes for ELEANOR ANN McNAIR:
Occupation: Teacher
Church Affiliation: Presbyterian
Fluent in several languages
Excellent businesswoman
Raised horses

More about ELEANOR ANN McNAIR:
Burial: February 1888, Hartley Cemetery, Lakeport, California
 Children of MARTIN HAMMACK and ELEANOR McNAIR are:

i. JOHN M³ HAMMACK, b. 1824, New Hope, Lincoln, Missouri.

3. ii. BRICE MARTIN HAMMACK, b. 23 January 1825, New Hope, Lincoln, Missouri; d. 17 August 1865, Near Finley, Lake County, California.

4. iii. MARY JANE HAMMACK, b. 18 November, New Hope, Lincoln, Missouri; d. 1907, Lake County, California.

5. iv. MAFGARET ANN HAMMACK, B. 02 March 1831, New Hope, Lincoln County, Missouri; d. 16 June 1889, Lake County, California.

6. v. MARTH SUSAN HAMMACK, B. 17 April 1835, New Hope, Lincoln County, Missouri; d. 16 June 1889, Lake County, California.

> vi. WILLIAM M. HAMMACK, b. 1838, Lincoln County, Missouri; d. Lake County, California.
> Notes for WILLIAM M. HAMMACK:
> William (Will) Hammack never married.
> vii. ROBERT JASPER HAMMACK, B. MARCH 1842, Lincoln County, Missouri; d. Lake County, California
> Notes for ROBERT JASPER HAMMACK:
> Robert Jasper Hammack never married.
> More about ROBERT JASPER HAMMACK:
> Burial: Lake County, California

7. viii. SARAH ELEANOR HAMMACK, B. 30 March 1845, Playberry, Lincoln County, Missouri; d. 14 January 1923, Lakeport, Lake County, California.

Generation No. 3

3. BRICE MARTIN[3] HAMMACK, (*MARTIN*[2] *DANIEL*[1]) WAS BORN 23RD of January 1825 in New Hope, Lincoln, Missouri, and died 17 August 186[5] in Near Finley, Lake County, California. He marrie

ELIZABETH ANN GRAY 25 December 1852 at her parent's home in Lincoln County, Missouri. She was born 08 March 1831.

More about BRICE MARTIN HAMMACK:
Burial: Hartley Cemetery, Lakeport, California

Children of BRICE HAMMACK and ELIZABETH GRAY are:

 i. SARA ELEANOR[4] HAMMACK, b. 31 May 1854.

8. ii. MARTHA ANNA HAMMACK, b. 23 November 1856.
 iii. HENRY MARTIN HAMMACK, b. 05 January 1859.

9. iv. GEORGE WASHINGTON HAMMACK, b. 15 December 1864

4. MARY JANE[3] HAMMACK (*MARTIN[2], DANIEL[1]*) WAS BORN 18 November in New hope, Lincoln, Missouri, and died 1907 in Lake County, California. She married EBENEZER BUCKINGHAM BOLE 22 August 1858 in Lake County, California.
More about MARY JANE HAMMACK:
Burial: 1907, Kelseyville Cemetery, Lake County, California
Children of MARY HAMMACK and EBENEZER BOLE are:

 i. ALBERT G.[4] BOLE.

ii. HARRIET A. BOLE.

iii. MARY ELLEN BOLE.

iv. FRANCIS A. BOLE.

v. WILLIE BOLE.

vi. MARTHA J. BOLE.

5. MARGARET ANN[3] HAMMACK (MARTIN[2,] DANIEL[1]) was born 02 March 1831 in New Hope, Lincoln County, Missouri, and died 28 April 1912 in Lakeport, Lake County, California. She married WOODS CRAWFORD 13 October 1852 in New Hope, Lincoln County, Missouri.

More about MARGARET ANN HAMMACK:

Burial: 1912, Hartley Cemetery, Lakeport, California

Children of MARGARET HAMMACK and WOODS CRAWFORD are:

    i. FLORENCE H.[4] CRAWFORD.

    ii. CROCKETT M CRAWFORD.

    iii. SUSAN R. CRAWFORD.

    iv. MARY L. CRAWFORD.

    v. EMMA P. CRAWFORD.

    vi. FRANK CRAWFORD.

6. MARTHA SUSAN[3] HAMMACK (*MARTIN[2]*, *DANIEL[1]*) was born 17 April 1835 in New Hope, Lincoln Co., Missouri, and died 16 June 1889 in Lake County, California. She married JONAS INGRAM June 1854 in Napa City, Napa, California. He was born 17 April 1823 in Jackson County, Illinois.

More about MARTHA SUSAN HAMMACK:
Burial: Kelseyville Cemetery, Lake County, California

Marriage Notes for MARTHA HAMMACK and JONAS INGRAM:
Martha Hammack and Jonas Ingram were the first white marriage in the Lake then Napa County. They traveled to Napa by horseback to be married.

Children of MARTHA HAMMACK and JONAS INGRAM are:
10. i. MARY ELLEN[4] INGRAM, b. 09 November 1862.
　　ii. CHARLES LEROY INGRAM, b. 10 July 1856.
　　iii. ELIZABETH INGRAM, b. 09 September 1858.
　　iv. HENRY INGRAM, b. 24 September 1860; m. BETTY.
　　v. SUSAN INGRAM, b. 07 April 1865.
　　vi. MARGARET FRANCIS INGRAM, b. 12 February 1867.
　　vii. BELLE INGRAM, b. 19 OCTOBER 1871.
　　ix. MARTHA INGRAM, b. 28 February 1873.
　　x. BABY INGRAM, b. 08 November 1876.

7. SARAH ELEANOR[3] HAMMACK (MARTIN[2], DANIEL[1]) was born 30 March 1845 in Playberry, ⌐incoln Co., Missouri, and died 14 January 1923 in

Lakeport, Lake County, California. She married WILLIAM MONORE WOODS December 1881

More about SARAH ELEANOR HAMMACK:
Burial: January 1923, Hartley Cemetery, Lakeport, California

Children of SARAH HAMMACK and WILLIAM WOODS are:
  i. CLARA[4] WOODS
  ii. JIM WOODS

Generation No. 4

8. MARTHA ANNA[4] HAMMACK (BRICE MARTIN[3], MARTIN[2], DANIEL[1]) was born 23 November 1856. She married JOHN SMITH EAKLE.
Child of MARTHA HAMMACK AND JOHN EAKLE is:
  i. ANNA ELIZABETH[5] EAKLE, m. WILSON STRAWN.

9. GEORGE WASHINGTON[4] HAMMACK (BRICE MARTIN[3,] MARTIN[2,] DANIEL[1]) WAS BORN 15 December 1864. He married MINNIE SPECT.

Children of GEORGE HAMMACK and MINN˙ SPECT are:
  i. MAE[5] HAMMACK.

ii. HERBERT HAMMACK.

iii. VALENTINE HAMMACK.

iv. CLAIR HAMMACK.

v. MERLE HAMMACK.

10. MARY ELLEN[4] INGRAM (MARTHA SUSAN[3], HAMMACK, MARTIN[2,] DANIEL[1]) was born 09 November 1862. She married JAMES MADISON REEVES. He was born 17 September 1849 in Wisconsin, and died 23 March 1927.

More about JAMES MADISON REEVES:
Burial: Kelseyville Cemetery, Lake County, California

Children of MARY INGRAM and JAMES REEVES are:
 i. HARRY LEROY[5] REEVES, b. Finley, California; d. 03 September, Lakeport, California; m. WILAMINNA ADELLE OTTE; b. 16 January 1886, Germany:
 ii. d. 23 September 1930, Big Valley, Lake County, California.

More about HARRY LEROY REEVES:
Burial: Kelseyville Cemetery, Lake County, California

Notes for WILAMINNA ADELLE OTTE:
Vilaminna Addelle Otte's nickname was Minna.

Minna died of Pulmonary Tuberculosis.

More about WILAMINNA ADELLE OTTE:
Burial: 25 September 1930, IOOF Cemetery, Kelseyville, Lake County, California

iii. ADA MARGARET REEVES, m. DICK GOTCHKISS.
iv. DORA REEVES, m. ROY WELLS.
v. RUTH REEVES, m. HARRY COULTER.
VINA REEVES, m. (1) UNKNOWN MEADOWS; m. (2) LLOYD CLARK: m. (3) CLYDE TABBERT.

CHAPTER THIRTY ONE

MAJOR BRICE MARTIN

Revolutionary War Army Officer, Virginia planter, husband, father, and devoted son. Brice was the son of the Immigrant Martin ancestor, Joseph Martin, Sr., from Bristol, England. He was born in Albemarle County, Virginia and owned a large farm on the west side of Smith River, a short distance from his brother, General Joseph Martin's "Scuffle Hill Farm" approximately two miles southwest of Martinsville.

Brice was described as tall, muscular and very active. He had dark hair; first married Unity Barksdale, and after her death he married Rachel Lucas, sister of Sarah Lucas, 1st wife of General Joseph Martin. Unity Barksdale and Major Brice had two sons, Joseph and William. Both these sons eventually migrated to Livingston, Tennessee in about 1810 where they ᵣed and died in Overton County. William died ᵣroximately the time of his father, close to year

1819. Joseph was still living in Tennessee in 1840. A court settlement in Tennessee reveals the children of William were in this order: Unity married Thomas Smith, Thomas married Jane McClendon, Brice married Mary Jane Burris, John B. married Matilda Holliman, and Joseph married Celina Watson. Major Brice's other son Joseph, b. 19 June, 1778, m. 15 November, 1809, d. 28 July 1830, Clay County, Tennessee. He married Ruth White; they had ten children as follows: Bethail, m. Creed T. Huddeleston, Brice Edward, m. Sarah Harrison, William W., no marriage, Eunice B., m. John Hansford, Robert Milton (RM), m. Ann Marchbanks. George W., no marriage, Milton E. m. #1- Eliza Watson, #2-Elizabeth Burris, Rachel Lucas #1-W.B. Chowning, #-2, John Riley. Joseph Martin, B. 12 August, 1830, d. 27 August, 1831. All buried in Overton or Clay County, Tennessee.

Major Brice Martin traveled on many frontier expeditions with his brother General Joseph Martin and his nephew, Colonel William Lucas Martin. Major Brice was also instrumental in establishing Martin's Station with his brother, General Joseph Martin, at Rose Hill, Virginia, twenty miles east of Cumberland Gap, Tennessee, an area called Powell's Valley. Many stories have been told, several books and manuscripts have been written about Cumberland Gap which served as a strategic crossroads during the American Revolution and also during the Civil War. General Joseph Martin was leader of the Powell's Valley expedition and eventual establishment

Martin's Station in 1775, which led to the opening of the Cumberland Gap, the gateway into Kentucky. It's estimated that more than 200,000 pioneers went into Kentucky and the Ohio Valley through Cumberland Gap to established new frontiers and new lives after the establishment of Martin's Station.

Major Brice Martin was named after a Family owned ship, "The Brice" in which their father came to America in 1725. The name has since been a family name. During one of the expeditions, he took up lands under Henderson & Company in Powell's Valley, near Beaver Dam Creek, some 8 miles from Martin's Station. Brice was at Long Island by the Holston River with his brother, General Joseph Martin. In 1802, he or his nephew of the same name was one of the surveyors to the Tennessee and Virginia Boundary Commission.

He shared the hardships of the settlers and protected them with a company of Rangers under his command. He was sometimes stationed in a fort, and often times pursuing marauding Indians. Brice opened channels of travel by which the 200,000 plus emigrants could more easily reach the newly forming frontier settlements (especially those going to Kentucky and Ohio Valley) by way of Martin's Station located near Cumberland Gap, Tennessee, stopping to resupply at Martin's Station. Virginia reconstructed the fort in 2003 and today it's the only authentic 1775 Fort in America. Built to 1775 specifications and each year during the second week of May, Wilderness Road State Park has a three day event, called "Raid at Martin's Station". Some years the Martin Families gather to have a "Nationwide Martin and Related Families Reunion".

$\mathcal{C}$HAPTER $\mathcal{T}$HIRTY $\mathcal{T}$WO

MAJOR BRICE MARTIN

Military Record

Brice's military experiences are given in several Virginia magazines and from Pittsylvania and Henry County records as follows:

- Through years of 1769, 1774 & 1775, Brice accompanied his brother, Captain (General) Joseph Martin, Jr. to Powell Valley, Southwestern Virginia in the attempt to establish a fort, later known as Martin's Station, today "Wilderness Road State Park", Ewing, Virginia, eight miles east of Cumberland Gap, Tennessee.

- Brice was in the battle at Point Pleasant, October 10, 1774 along with his brother John Martin and his nephew, Colonel William

Lucas Martin; all were under the command of Colonel Andrew Lewis.

- Brice took the "Oath of Allegiance" to the Commonwealth of Virginia, renouncing his allegiance to Great Britain on August 30, 1777.

- Cherokee Expedition—August 25, 1776 through March 7, 1777.

- Fort Patrick Henry—1776 through year 1777.

- Frontiers of Fincastle County, Virginia; July 1, 1776 through August 31, 1776. (Today Lee County)

- Rye Cove on the Clinch River, Virginia, February 1 through March 31, 1777.

- Washington County, Virginia. Rye Cove— May 1 to June 30, 1777.

- Brice was Captain of the Henry County Militia and licensed to keep an ordinary at the courthouse, Henry County, Virginia. John Barksdale was appointed 2nd Lt. under Captain Brice.

- In 1781, Brice received orders to march his Militia Company to Hillsborough, North Carolina to prepare for the Battle of Guilford Courthouse which was one of the last battle and the turning point against British forces of the Revolutionary War. With this battle and the battle of Kings Mountain it nearly devastated the British Forces. Thirteen months later the British surrendered at Yorktown.

- In 1782, Brice was commissioned as Major by Governor Benjamin Harrison of Virginia.

After the death of his wife, Unity Barksdale, he married Rachel Lucas on August 7, 1793 in Orange County, Virginia. Brice died at his farm on the West side of Smith River, Henry County, Martinsville, Virginia in 1818- 1919. (*Rachel was the sister of Sarah Lucas, wife of General Joseph Martin). Major Brice was the youngest son of Captain Joseph Martin Sr. and Susannah (Chiles) Martin, who was a descendant of the prominent family of Walter Chiles Jr. Major Brice was the last of the brothers, George, who remained in Albemarle as a farmer, married and had two daughters. Captain William married Rachel Dalton and lived out the remainder of his life in Stokes County and both are buried at the Hughesville cemetery, below Martinsville. Many have confused Captain William with his son General William Martin who died in Tennessee, and also get him confused with another Captain William Peters Martin of Caroline County. Captain William Peters Martin was a son of John Martin Jr. an attorney whose father was Colonel John Martin who went to Ireland in about 1756. General Joseph, the middle son, became a farmer, long hunter; soldier at fifteen with George Washington's Army at Pittsburg, and later became a Captain in the Virginia Militia. Then in 1777 was appointed the Cherokee Agent, by the Continental Congress, Virginia and North Carolina to deal with the Cherokee Nation. He was also North Carolina's Brigadier General during that same time. He held the post of Cherokee Agent from 1777–1789, the longest serving agent in history. He returned to his family and home in Henry County, became a Virginia Representative for another 12 years, and his last duty, at the request of the War Department, was to go to visit the Cherokee Nation and check on the welfare of the Cherokees. He went to the Nation with his long time servant Toby and likely visited his Cherokee family, daughter and son. Nancy, who married Michael Hildebrand and raised twelve children, lived east of Cleveland. His son James C. Martin had a small farm in the same area and also worked for Chief Vann in Georgia at his store. James eventually immigrated to Indian Territory in 1837 and settled in Going Snake District (Today Adair County, Oklahoma). It's speculated that he may have gone with his first cousin, Judge John Martin Jr. and his two wives, Nellie and Lucy (McDaniel) Martin and their 16 children. John Jr. became the First Cherokee Nation Supreme Court Justice Tahlequah, the Cherokee Nation Headquart After General Joseph returned from his visit t

Cherokee Nation in the area, southwest of Knoxville down to Cleveland, and Chattanooga Tennessee, a journey of two to three month months, and upon returning to his farm on Leatherwood Creek, near Martinsville on 11 December, he was sick and went to bed. He died seven days later on 18 December, 1808 of a stroke. He was buried with Masonic and Military Honors in the family cemetery beside Leatherwood Creek, along with about 35 family members.

Martinsville, Virginia was named in honor
of General Joseph Martin in 1791.

Brother, John became an Indian Trader in the Cherokee Nation, marrying a 1/8 Cherokee women, Susannah Emory. They had three children, Rachel, Nancy and John Sr. John later became the Eastern Cherokee Nation's Secretary Treasurer, a Judge and helped write the Cherokee Constitution, and helped ʼayout the new town of the New Eschota in Georgia. ʼhn Sr. owned a Licensed Trading Post near the ʼrokee Scared Town of Chota. His son, John Jr.

1/8 Cherokee, became the first Cherokee Supreme Court Justice, after immigrating to Indian Territory (Oklahoma) in 1837 with his entire family of both wives, and sixteen children. Today he has descendants all over the nation, who have distinguished themselves as doctors, lawyers, politicians, educators, ranchers and farmers.

Major Brice, whose military record is recorded among these pages, remained with General Joseph from 1777 to 1789. Brice served at a Fort sometimes but mostly on in the wilderness frontier. He died in 1819 near Martinsville, Virginia on his farm.

CHAPTER THIRTY THREE

MARTIN SURNAME HISTORY

Martin is a Norman name meaning "Warlike". It's mentioned in the "Rolls of the Battle of Abbey" where our ancestor General William Martin from Tours, France fought. He was the Captain of the 40+ ships and was "William the Conquers" Army General. They sailed to England from France and overthrew the King of England in 1066AD. "William the Conquer" became the King after the Battle of Hastings.

For General William Martin's share and compensation for his service, he was given the Barony of Cemmeas of Kemeys County, Pembroke and he became Baron of Kemeys and Lord of Comber Martin of Martinshoe, in Devon.

General William Martin's son, Baron Robert Fitz Martin, married Maude Perverell. Robert Fitz and Maude Perverell Martin owned the Newport/Martin stle in Wales not far from Bristol, England. William

Martin II, Baron of Darlington was born in 1160AD, from whom all those of English lineage bear the name Martin.

General William Martin is the earliest known ancestor of our Martin family.

The Newport/Martin Castle today is a private residence but may be opened to the public soon. You can view pictures of the castle, cemetery and surrounding grounds on the following website.

CHAPTER THIRTY FOUR

MARTIN FAMILY HISTORY

In 1066AD the Martin Family was living in France. Our early ancestor, William Martin was a General and Captain of ships for William the Conqueror who sailed to England on October 14, 1066AD where the Battle of Hastings was fought. William the Norman, who later was known as "William the Conquer", was the winner of the Battle of Hastings and became King of England. A roll was prepared with the names and titles of the Norman chivalry that had followed Williams' banner. This was the famous "Roll of Battle or Battle Abbey". It was dedicated to St. Martin who was the son of a Roman military tribune in Hungary. The festival of St. Martin was instituted and casks of new wines were tapped. Our English ancestors kept the feast by eating roasted goose. Some still celebrate this feast today on November, 11th of each year.

1208AD—In the reign of King John in the town

of Newport, Wales, was incorporated by a charter granted by William Martin. Newport castle, founded by Martin de Tours, is believed to have been completed by his great-grandson, Sir William Martin, son of William Martin who married the daughter of Lord Rhys Gryffidith, Prince of South Wales.

Middle 1600's—William Martin of Bristol, England was born at the Manor of Pindergast in Pembroke County, England about the middle of the 17th Century. This manor and estate of his father passed onto the eldest son and William, being a younger son, entered the mercantile business in Bristol. He carried on an extensive American trade. At this time Bristol was the second city in the Kingdome in size.

Children of William Martin of Bristol are:

1. George—Succeeded his father as merchant in Bristol.

2. Nancy—No history available.

3. John—No history available.

4. Joseph, Sr., was sent to America on a family owned ship, "The Brice". After several Atlantic crossings the ship disappeared from records never to be heard of again. Joseph Sr. married into the prominent Walter Chiles family of Jamestown, Virginia and later purchased two large farms in 1737 near Charlottesville, Albemarle County, Virginia. Living th

remainder of his life there, Joseph, Sr. and Susannah raised 5 sons and 6 daughters.

In 1725 (Generation I) —Joseph Sr. came to America. In England, he was about to enter into an undesirable marriage, according to his father, William of Bristol, so he sent Joseph on one of his shipping vessels, "The Brice" to Virginia. Joseph was given to the "tender passion" for he soon fell in love with and married Susannah Chiles, the daughter of one of the oldest and most respected families in Jamestown. Joseph is described as a perfect English gentleman, possessing all the arrogance and self-important air, characteristic of them as a nation. He was bold, self-willed and had a high sense of honor. His wife, Susannah, was described as a "most amiable woman." She is described by a grandson Colonel William Lucas Martin, as the "best of womankind." Her parents were English and had a large family, all highly respected, as well as the offspring of the prominent families of Waller, Chiles, Carr, Lewis, Overton and Terry families of Virginia.

After the death of his wife, Susannah (Chiles) Martin, Joseph married again to Ann P. Sandige. He died in Albemarle County, Virginia in 1760 leaving a large estate.

CHAPTER THIRTY FIVE

CHILDREN OF CAPTAIN JOSEPH MARTIN SR. AND SUSANNAH (CHILES) MARTIN

Joseph Martin, Sr., (the immigrant to America) and Susannah Chiles lived first in Orange County Virginia then moved to Albemarle County where he obtained two large farms about eight miles northwest of Charlottesville, Virginia. They became parents of five sons and six daughters listed below. Not necessarily in this order. The sons are listed first and it's believed this is their birth order.

1. George Martin, m. Mary "Polly" Durett. They had two daughters, Salley, b. ca. 1760/1763, d. 1778 m. Richard Flynt. Susannah Durrett, b. ca. 1765, m. Martin Burris. ca. 1780

2. Captain William Martin a Revolutionary Soldier who died in Stokes County, North Carolina, 1808 buried in Hughesville Cemetery, below Martinsville, Virginia. Married Rachel Dalton, daughter of Samuel Dalton and Ann Danridge Redd.

The names of their children were: Nancy, b. ca 1771, m. James Fulkinson, Sarah "Sallie" m. Captain John Hughes, Captain John Hughes, buried, 5 miles south of Franklin, Tennessee in General William Martin Cemetery. Virginia "Jiny", m. Samuel Clark #1, and Sampson Sawyer #2, Susannah Chiles, m. Reuben Moore.

Mary "Polly" m. William Moore. General William "Buck", never married. He moved to Tennessee in 1806. Was in the war of 1812, Battle of New Orleans, and Battle of Pensacola and served on staff of General Andrew Jackson.

Samuel, b. ca 1785, d. ca 1855, m. 10 January 1811 to Sarah "Sallie" Clement, Williamson County Tennessee. Several of their children went to Williamson County Tennessee, and some to Madison County North Carolina.

3. General Joseph Martin, Martinsville, Henry County, Virginia (City of Martinsville named in his honor in 1791, died December 18, 1808. He is buried at the family Cemetery on

Leatherwood Creek, Martinsville, Virginia. General Joseph Martin was married three times and had twenty children. #1, Sarah Lucas, seven children, #2, Elizabeth "Betsy" Ward, two children, #3, Susannah Graves, eleven children. Some say he was married as many as five times but recent research from several noted genealogist have proven he had only three wives and twenty children. For further information contact: General Joseph Martin Association, 308 North Riata Street, Gilbert, Arizona, 85234. You may also seek information at:
******JoeMartinProperties@cox.net******

4. John Martin Sr, Indian Fur Trader went to Cherokee Nation about 1777, the same year his brother Gen Joseph martin was appointed Agent of the Cherokees at Long Island. He married Susannah Emory granddaughter of Ludovic Grant. John Sr. and Susannah Emory (1/8 Cherokee) had three children. One son later became Judge John Martin Jr. who was the Secretary-Treasurer of the Cherokee Nation and First Chief Court Justice, and helped in laying out the Cherokee Town of New Eschota, Georgia. He was a circuit judge for two Cherokee districts. He was reelected the First Cherokee Supreme Court Justice after

immigrating west to Indian Territory in 1837 with his family, today Tahlequah, Oklahoma. Judge John died on October 17, 1840 at Fort Gibson, Oklahoma and is buried there.

He married Nellie and Lucy McDaniel who were sisters, each had eight children. Today these descendants can be found nationwide.

5.   Major Brice Martin, Henry County, Martinsville, Virginia, owned, the Revolutionary War Rifle, the subject of this book. It is now on display at the Lakeport County Museum in Lakeport California. The rifle was donated by a descendant of the Hammack family who migrated from Lincoln County, Missouri in 1853 arriving in California in April 1854.

To this union of Joseph Sr. and Susannah Chiles Martin, in addition to the five sons mentioned, there were six daughters born to this marriage as follows: Susannah, Mary, Sarah, Martha, Ann and Olive. Several of the daughters migrated to Henry County, Virginia and some went to Smith County, Dixon Springs, Tennessee, where General Joseph Martin's eldest son, Colonel William Lucas Martin lived.

1. Susannah, b. 19 February, 1737, m. 13 January 1761 to Henry Woody. d. 21 June 1835.

2. Mary (Nellie), married John Hammack Sr. and went to North Carolina, and after his death she moved the family to Dixon Springs, Tennessee.

3. Olive, m. Ambrose Edwards, 15 March 1774. Three children were: Brice Edwards, m. Martha Barksdale. Martha Edwards, m. Milton Ferney. John Edwards's m. Martha Johnson.

4. Sarah, m. Thomas Burris. Children were: Charles Burris, m. Elizabeth Dickenson. Martin Burris m. Susannah Martin, Susannah Martin Burris, m. Leonard Davis. Jestina Burris, m. Stanwix Hord.

5. Martha, m. Pomfort Waller Sr., Nancy Ann, m. Livingston Isbell, their children were: Susannah Chiles, m. Thomas Barlow. Francis Livingston, m. Ambrose Parks, Mary (Polly) m. James T. Brown, Nancy "Ann" m. Captain William Brown.

6. Nancy Ann, m. Livingston Isbell. Their children were: Susannah Chiles, m. Thomas Barlow. Francis Livingston, m. Ambrose Parks. Mary M. (Polly) m. James M. Brown. Nancy "Ann" m. Captain William Brown, 6 September, 1801, Wilkes, North Carolina. Children were: Livingston I, Mary, m. William M. Parks, Nancy

m. George I. Black, Jesse Franklin, m. Phoebe Parks. Joseph Martin Brown, b. 2 August, 1811, Wilkes, NC. d. 23 January, 1896, Effingham, Illinois. Wade Hampton, b. 17 August, 1815, d. 15 July 1869. m. Amanda Caldwell, 11 January, 1835.

CHAPTER *Thirty Six*

WILL OF MAJOR BRICE MARTIN

Written & Typed Will of Brice Martin

Henry County, Martinsville, Virginia

File #7585, Pt. 3—031956
Will Book, # 1—1777—1799,
Will Book, #2— 1799—1820,
Henry County, Virginia

P. 135— I, Brice Martin, of the County of Henry, State of Virginia, do hereby make my last will and testament in manner and form following, that is to say: I give to my beloved wife all my real and personal estate to be hers during her life and that she shall be at liberty of disposing of my negro girl Chancy, at her pleasure.

Item—I give and bequeath unto my son Joseph Martin, my negro man Will and his wife Winney and their Children, to Wit: Tom, George, Mary, Major, and

Sarah, to him and his heirs forever, from and after the death of my wife above mentioned.

Item—I give and bequeath unto the heirs of my deceased son William Martin three Negroes to Wit: Bob, Judah and Warren to them and their heirs forever.

Item—After the death of my wife it is my wish for my land to be sold to the highest bidder and the money arising from the sale to be divided between my son Joseph and the heirs of my deceased son William, as to make the portion fully equal with the portion which I have bequeathed to each legatee.

Item—It is my desire that after the death of my wife, all the perishable parts of my estate also be sold and equally divided between my son Joseph and the heirs of my son William, deceased. Lastly, I appoint my friend Thomas East and John Barksdale my Executors to this, my last will and testament hereby revoking all others or former wills or testaments by me heretofore make. In Witness whereof I have here unto set my hand and affixed my seal this twenty first day of December in the year of our lord Christ one thousand eight hundred and eighteen.

Brice X Martin

Witnesses:
John Turner
Mary Turner
Nancy Turner
Proved, 8 March 1819.

Brice Martin's hand written and typed will, proved 8 Mar. 1819, after his death.

CHAPTER THIRTY SEVEN

WILL OF RACHEL (LUCAS) MARTIN-WIFE OF MAJ. BRICE MARTIN

Will Books of Henry County, Virginia

Will Book —3, 1820 —1831, P. 203

I, Rachel Martin of the County of Henry and State of Virginia, do make and ordain this to be my last will and testament revoking all others.

Impremis: I will and bequeath unto the children of William Martin and Mary, his wife, son of my late husband, Brice martin the following Negroes: Bob, Nan, Lucy and Anthony and their increase to them and their heirs forever.

Item—I will and appoint John Barksdale, Executor of this my last will and testament. In witness, where of I have here unto set my hand and affixed my seal, this 4th day of November 1822.

Rachal her X Martin mark

Witnesses:
John Barksdale, Brice Edwards,
Mary Turner

CHAPTER THIRTY EIGHT

CONCLUSION

This concludes some of the history and origin of the Hammack family, the overland journey to California and the first white settlement of Lake County by the Martin Hammack party in 1854. As has been the experience and history of the pioneers and early settlers of this country the land settled and acquired by the members of the Hammack party, with two exceptions, has through the years passed into other ownership than that of the descendants of the original settlers and owners. With the disposal of the original homesteads and changing conditions, most of the descendants of the Hammack Families have left Lake County, possibly forever, and with the passing of a few generations, it is probable that only the name will survive with Lake County as a historical fact of the original settlement of the County. Only five Hammack descendant and related families have been found, that still have ties to Lake County, California.

The majority of this family history, plus the overland journey record was passed down by Harold M. Hammack, dated January 20, 1939. No contact or family history from him has been found. I have taken the liberty to make corrections, changes where needed, and edited the original document.

The Hammack family lost two of its members to death during the journey. They had courage and determination, and for those that endured, a better life awaited them in the rich valleys of California.

As to actual events and people, this book attempts to relate the true story of one family to make a better life for themselves, and it seems it was the right choice.

If this book connects a relative of either a Martin or Hammack family living today or creates a desire to dig deeper into their family history, or perhaps your own, I cannot ask for a greater reward.

$\mathcal{A}$CKNOWLEDGEMENT

This is the first book to give historical record of the Journey of Old Fremont and the Hammack families in authentic text and pictures.

I am especially indebted to my sources for their quality contribution. My gratitude is recorded here with, to the following contributors:

1. June (Martin) Wells, Plainview, Texas – Major Brice Martin Descendant

2. Dr. Lyman C. Draper, Historian

3. Dr. Stephen B. Weeks

4. Linda L. (Golter) Martin

5. William Kent Martin, Mays, Oklahoma – General Joseph Martin Descendant

6. John Thomas (J.T.) Martin, Chesapeake, Virginia - General Joseph Martin Descendant

7. Harold M. Hammack, Riverside, California – Hammack Descendant

8. Jennifer (Hammack) Howard, Azalea, Oregon.

9. Melinda & Bob Horanda, Lakeport, California – Martin Descendant

10. Albemarle County Will Books, Charlottesville, Virginia.

11. Henry County Will Books, Martinsville, Virginia.

12. The Virginia Magazine

13. Lincoln County, Missouri, Heritage Record Researchers

14. Napa County, California 1860 Census

15. Lake County Museum, Lakeport, California

16. Ellen Humble, Colusa, California – Hammack Descendant

17. Frederick Smoot – Trails West

18. Kella Jones – Typist

19. Bob Hughes, Jackson Tennessee, General Joseph Martin descendant.

20. University of Oregon

21. Daniel (Dan) A. Martin

$\mathcal{S}$UMMARY

This is a portrayal of a family of seven, along with eighteen other members of a wagon train who headed west from New Hope, Lincoln County, Missouri to California over the Santa Fe Trail. Little did the family know of the adventure that would forever change their lives. They were seeking adventure, land and a new future plus a new life in a faraway place. Not only did they endure the hardships of wagon train travel, the harsh elements of the weather, desert heat, and mountains, but they also faced an unknown journey through lands of the Plains Indians. For this, they hoped to receive the rich rewards of a new home and a better life. This is an account of their successful six month journey to Lake County, California arriving in April 1854.

The descendants became well known as successful business owners, attorneys and farmers. Today the Hammack descendants are lost, except for three families in Oregon, Washington, California, three families in California, and one in Georgia, Ellen Humble. Ellen Humble gave me valuable family history of the Hammack families. She lived in

Williams & Colusa California most of her life and furnished hundreds of names, dates and family history information to the author of this book which I'm eternally grateful.

$\mathcal{A}$BOUT $\mathcal{T}$HE $\mathcal{A}$UTHOR

Colonel Joe L. Martin is an Air Force Retired Colonel and resides in Arizona with his wife, Linda, after living in several states and two years in Japan. He is a pilot, a definite traveler, adventurer and serious genealogist who leaves no stones unturned in searching for his ancestors who helped shaped this nation during the American Revolution and through the western migration during the gold rush days of the mid 1800's. He is happiest when exploring the country's libraries, state archives and searching for additional family members scattered throughout the United States. He has authored one other book, "The Anthology of General Joseph Martin". General

Joseph is his fourth-great-grandfather who lived in Martinsville, Virginia.

Colonel Martin is a relative of John Hammack, Sr.'s wife, Nellie (Mary Martin), the mother of Martin, Brice, and John Jr. Hammack. Nellie was the daughter of Captain Joseph Martin, Sr., Colonel Martin's 5th Great Grandfather, of Albemarle County, Virginia, who died January 14, 1762. Martin Hammack's mother, Mary (Polly) Martin, was Colonel Martin's half, 3rd great-grad-aunt. Her husband was Daniel Hammack. She was the daughter of General Joseph Martin and Sarah Lucas Martin.